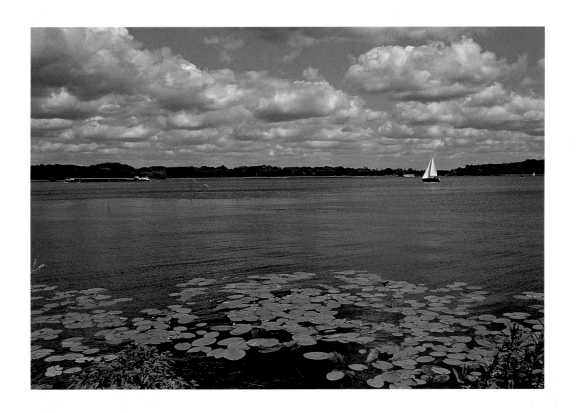

Journey through

BRANDENBURG

Photos by

Wolfgang Korall

Text by

Georg Schwikart

Stürtz

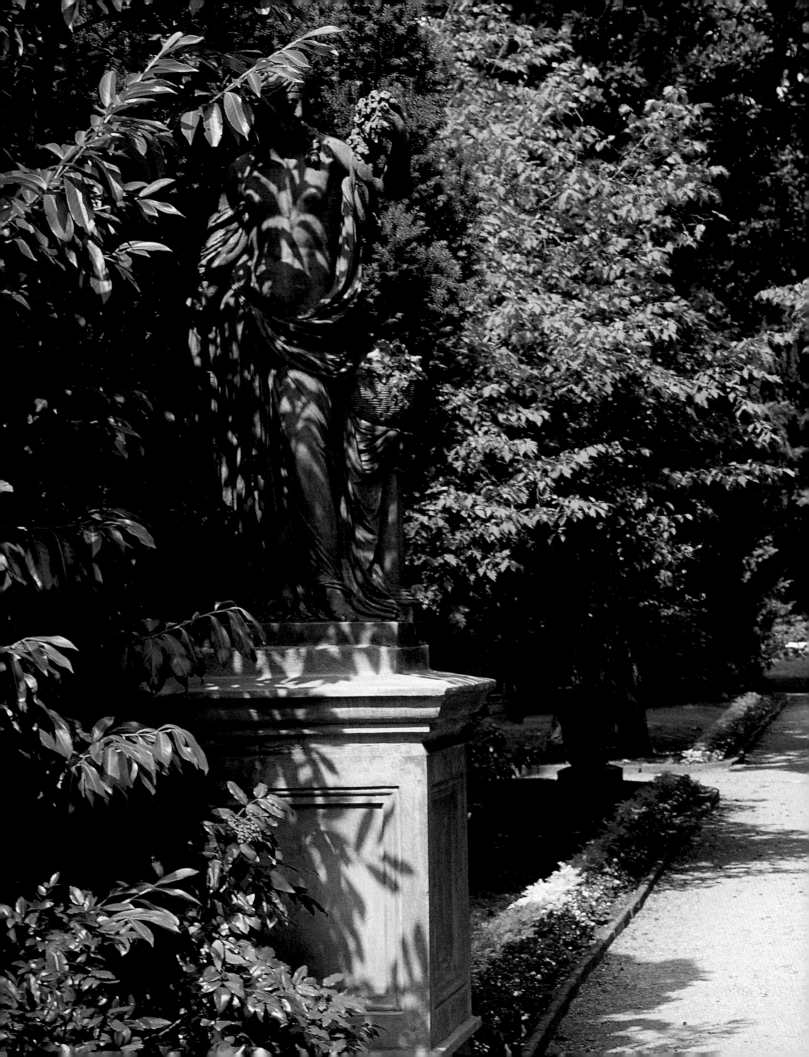

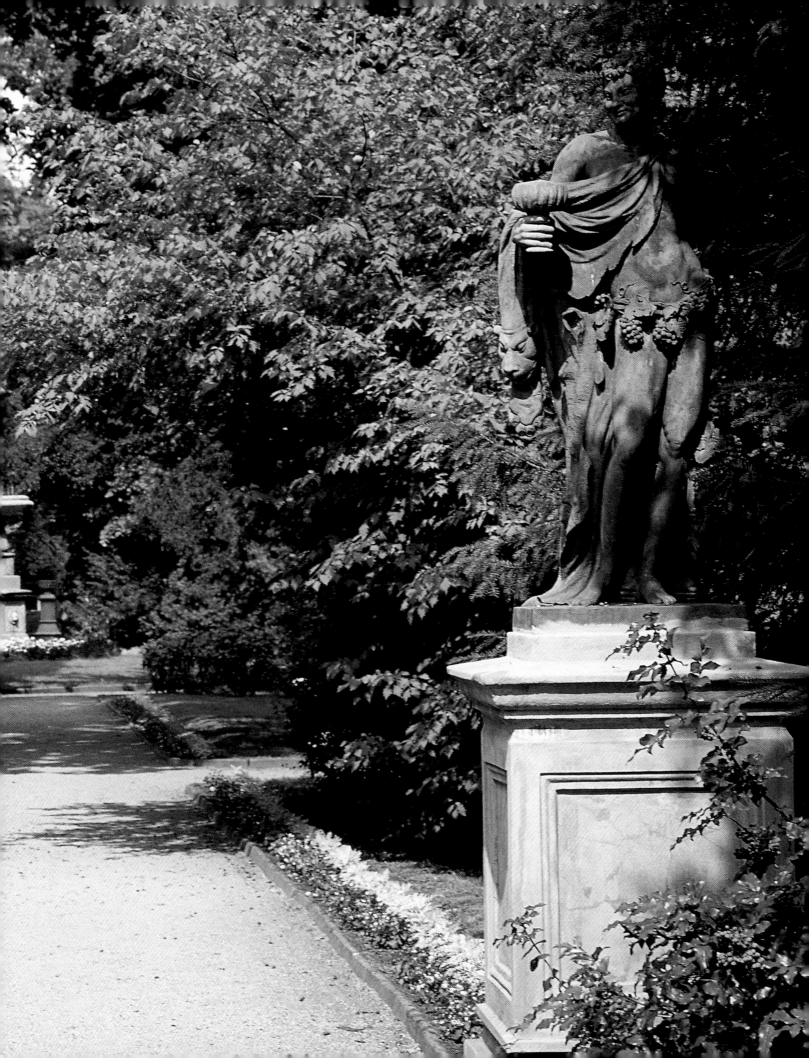

CONTENTS

First page:
Brandenburg is this lovely! Idyllic landscape on the Jungfern Lake by Potsdam. Who wouldn't want to sail along?

Previous page:
In the 18th century, it was the fashion to look back at ancient times wistfully. In Neuruppin, Crown Prince Frederick had a "temple" built and a temple garden set

around it in the Roman style. The architect Geor[g] Wenzeslaus von Knobel[s]dorff created his first work here. Later, the grounds were given some oriental accents. A secluded spot!

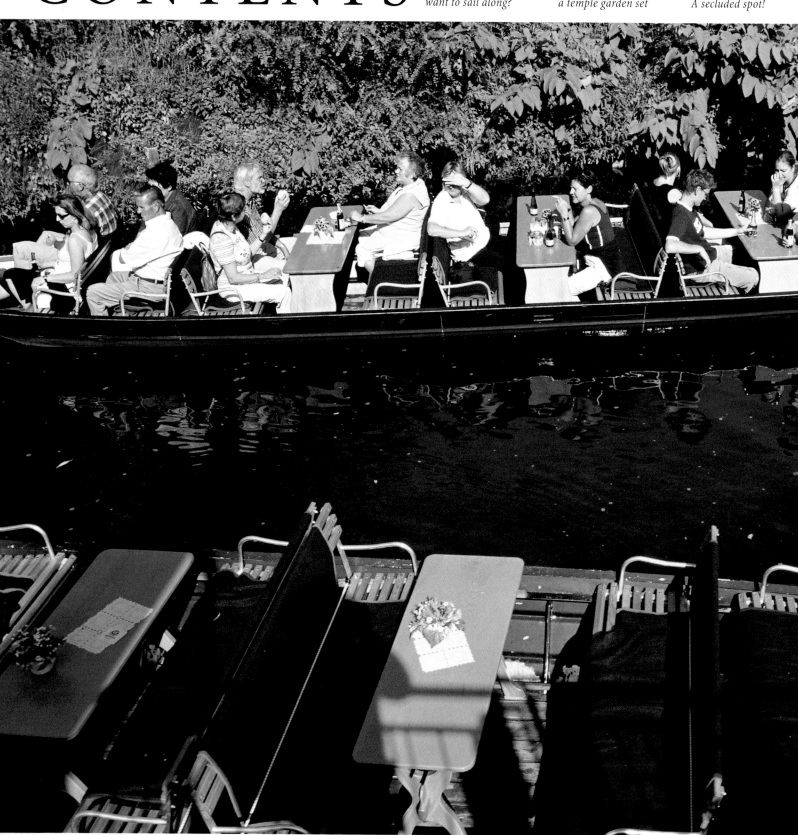

Below:
The marshy lowlands of
the middle Spree, from
Cottbus to south of
Lübben, form the Spree-
wald, a unique nature
reserve. Here, the Spree

has very little drop and
splits up into numerous
branches, which are per-
fectly suited for a leisurely
trip in a punt, like here
near Burg.

Pages 10/11:
Sanssouci is a World
Cultural Heritage Site.
Prince Louis Ferdinand
of Prussia, a descendant
of the palace builder
King Frederick II,
suitably assessed at the

beginning of the third
millennium: "Art meets
nature and history meets
art – a great, moving
triad that has been
audible for two and a
half centuries.

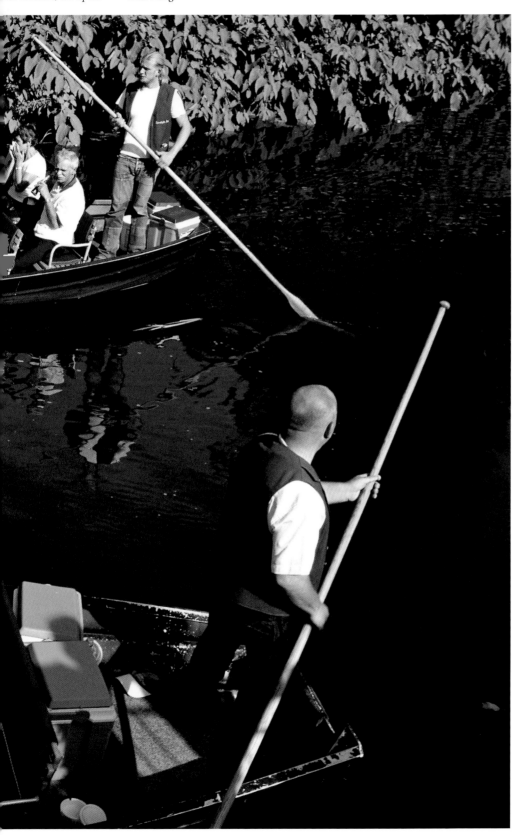

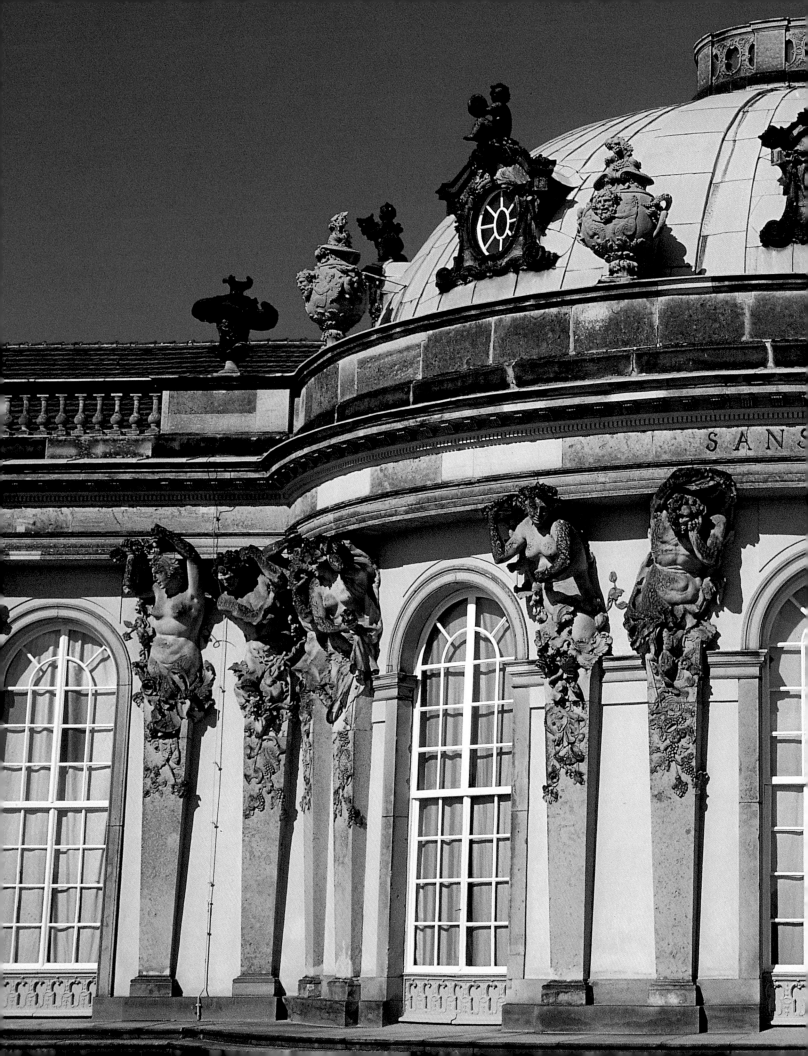

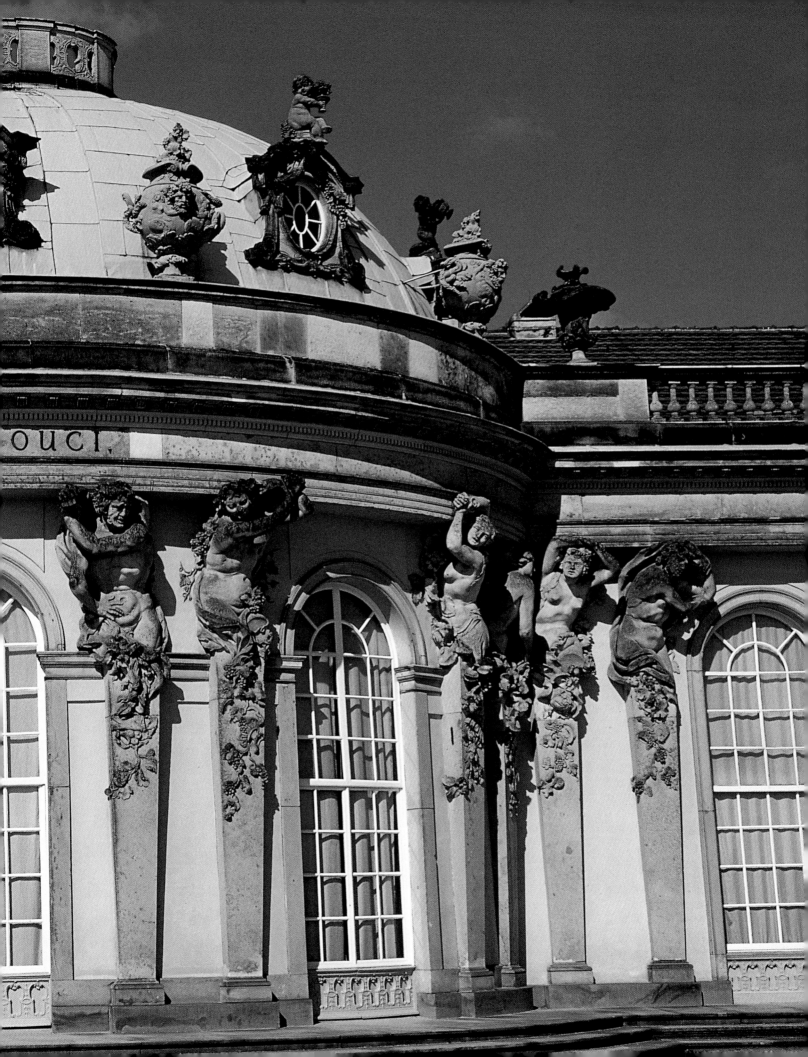

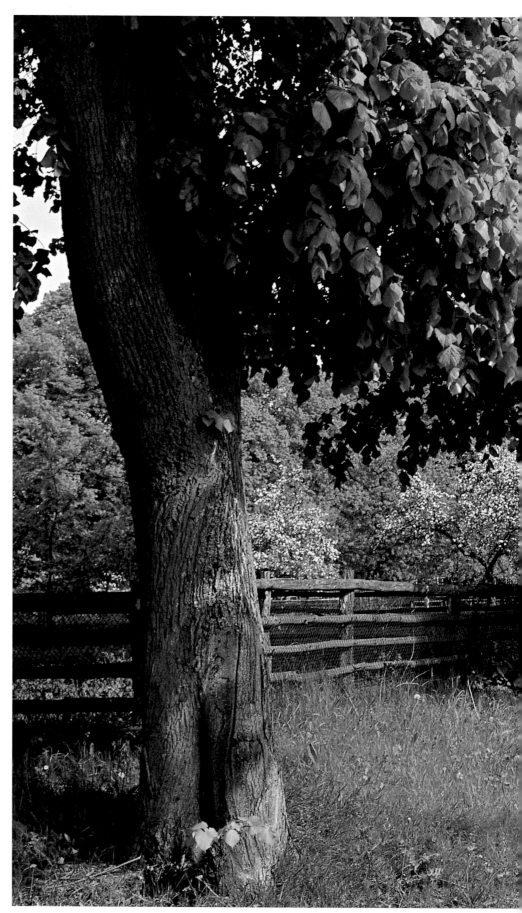

"A hundred year old avenue must be guarded and protected as one's own house; for even in modern times it will need another hundred years to grow. One does not give away riches such as this without resistance." (Günter de Bruyn) – The photo shows a row of trees near Küstrinchen.

When the autumn sun hangs low in the sky, it seems to be taking a final opportunity to show off its splendour. If you drive down a tree-lined avenue in this light, where here and there golden-yellow leaves loosen from the trees and float gently to the ground, it is like being showered with golden pennies. In the snow, the avenues are dreamlike landscapes; in the rain, they produce melancholy; in the fog, they hide a secret. In the spring, the full splendour of their white and red blossoms testifies to nature's zest for life.

Avenues are more than roads lined by rows of trees; they are, as someone expressed poetically, "the soft-focus lens on the harsh Brandenburg landscape." Many of the giant trees were planted as early as the 18th century, as road markers, givers of shade and shields from the wind. Approximately 12,000 kilometres (almost 7,500 miles) of these avenues crisscross "the Holy Roman Empire's box of sand," as the Mark Brandenburg was called – the term was allegedly coined by Luther – due to its barren, sandy soil.

Today's federal state of Brandenburg (the largest of the "new" states after German reunification in 1990) encompasses the landscapes of Prignitz, Uckermark, Neumark, Havelland, Mittelmark, Spreewald and Lower Lusatia. They stretch over approximately 30,000 square kilometres (11,600 square miles). This area is the home of about two and a half million people; their numbers are presently dwindling as people leave in search of jobs. They are fewer inhabitants than in Berlin, which Brandenburg surrounds. The 250-kilo-

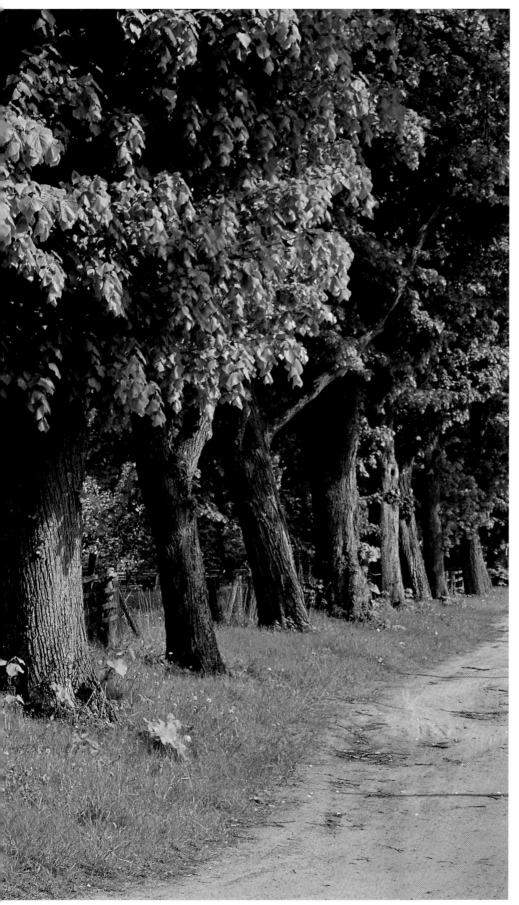

metre (155-mile) border to Poland gives Brandenburg the function of a bridge to the neighbouring country: in Guben and Frankfurt an der Oder, the former foes and now allied states are separated merely by a stroll across the Oder bridges.

ABODE OF WHALES AND HERRINGS

The Brandenburg Gate is known by all, having come to symbolize Germany. After its construction (1788–1791), it served as a border post in the city walls; whoever passed through it was in the Mark Brandenburg. Around 1800, Heinrich von Kleist (the most famous poet of the march after Theodor Fontane) described this landscape:

"It is as if this entire northern stretch of Germany has been destined by nature to remain the sea floor for ever and ever, and, as it were, the sea had only receded so far by accident, thus forming a tract of earth originally more meant as the abode of whales and herrings than of humans."

Perhaps the ancient Germanic peoples felt the same way; those who settled the region between the Oder and Elbe before the Common Era, only to move on during the migration of peoples. Slavs settled in the region from the 6th century CE. They erected a frontier fortress, the Brandenburg, on the river Havel. The eastern Frankish King Henry I conquered it in the winter of 928-929. In 948, his successor Otto I founded the bishopric of Brandenburg, hence giving the name "Brendanburg" its first written mention.

Over the ensuing centuries, the march changed owners many times: the Slavs were followed by the Ascanians, who were supplanted in the 14th and 15th centuries by Wittelsbach and Luxembourg rule, and finally in 1411 by the Hohenzollern, who remained the regents of the "box of sand" for over 500 years, until the end of the empire in 1918. Milestones in the history of Brandenburg in these times were the founding of the first university in 1506 in Frankfurt an der Oder and the adoption of the Reformation in 1539. During the Thirty Years' War from 1618 to 1648, the march became a battlefield and was badly devastated by marauding soldiers, by plundering and epidemics. Nearly half of the inhabitants perished; in some regions, such as Prignitz, Uckermark and Barnim, up to 90 percent were slain.

THE GREAT ELECTOR FREDERICK WILLIAM

In 1640, the "Great Elector" Frederick William took over regency. After the West-phalian Peace of 1648, he enlarged the army, the economy and the administration. He attempted to get the economy back on its feet by recruiting foreign settlers. From 1662 to 1669, the Oder-Spree Canal was con-structed, making Berlin a junction between Hamburg and Silesia. In 1675, the Swedish occupying forces were crushed in the Battle of Fehrbellin and driven from the march for good.

In 1685, the Great Elector enacted the Edict of Potsdam, offering the Huguenots, perse-cuted in France for their Protestant faith, freedom to settle in the march, and granting them privileges such as customs and tax ex-emption. By the year 1700, 20,000 religious refugees from France settled in Brandenburg, 6,000 of them in Berlin. They helped the march recover from the losses caused by the Thirty Years' War and lastingly influenced the culture and economy of the country. The Huguenots brought asparagus, cauliflower, peas and beans with them to Prussia and enriched the language with expressions such as "Bulette" from "boulette," (for rissole), "Manöver" from "manoeuvre" and "Mucke-fuck" – from "moka faux" (artificial mocha). Their descendants included Theodor Fontane as well as the many other people of Berlin and Brandenburg who still have French sur-names today.

In 1701, the pomp-loving son of the Great Elector, Elector Frederick III, crowned himself king in Prussia and had Berlin built up to an "Athens on the Spree." From then, Brandenburg was the central province of the ambitious state of Prussia. In 1721, Johann Sebastian Bach dedicated his "Brandenburg Concertos" to Frederick's youngest half-brother, Margrave Christian Ludwig von Brandenburg.

Frederick's extravagance provoked a state crisis. He died in 1713; his son, the "soldier king" Frederick William I, was more frugal. Under him, Prussia became a military power without him ever going to war. He prohibit-ed the "witch trials" and introduced general compulsory school attendance. He made Potsdam his second royal capital; the Dutch Quarter was built there. He had a number of houses built for his bodyguard regiment, the

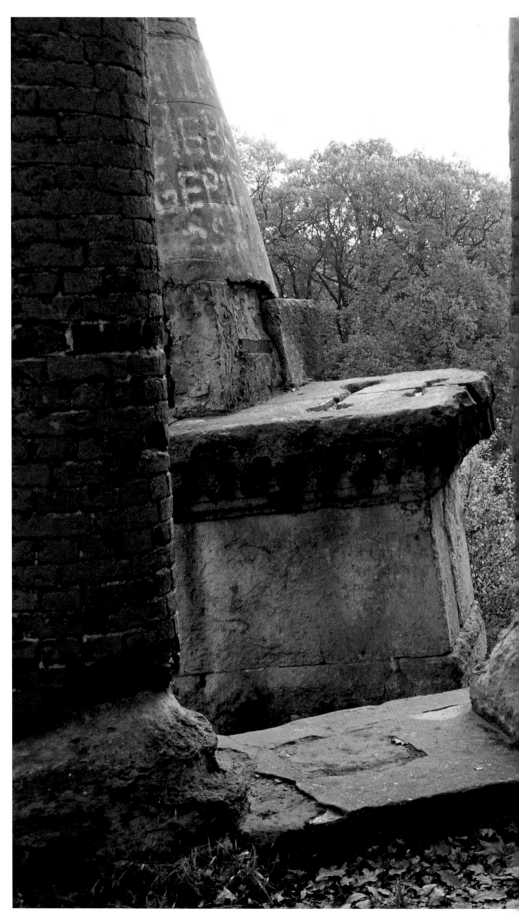

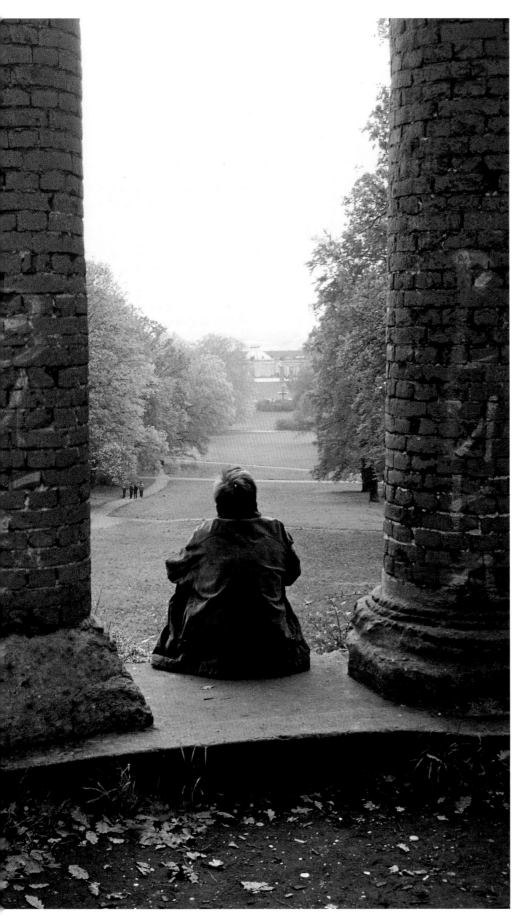

"Long Fellows." Recruited from throughout Europe, the regiment's grenadiers had to be at least six feet tall.

His son, the aesthete Frederick II, builder of the famous palace of Sanssouci, transformed Prussia into a major European power. Over 60,000 new inhabitants moved into the march. The Oderbruch – the landscape on the western shore of the Oder River – was drained and cultivated. Settlers were recruited from many different regions, from Hesse-Darmstadt, Mecklenburg, Saxony and Württemberg, but also from Lower Austria and French-speaking parts of Switzerland. Towns like Beauregard and Vevais were named by their French-speaking settlers.

After Prussia's defeat by France in 1806, the march was occupied by the conquerors. In 1813, the advance of the Napoleonic troops to Berlin failed, thus ending French dominion in the march. Following the Congress of Vienna in 1815, Brandenburg became a Prussian province; Lower Lusatia was added to it. In 1838, the first railway travelled between Berlin and Potsdam. In the 19th century, Brandenburg's population grew from one million to 3.3 million.

RAMBLES THROUGH THE MARK BRANDENBURG

No other German landscape has such a guide to its historical sites than the march: Theodor Fontane's *Rambles through the Mark Brandenburg* was published between 1862 and 1889. Far from any sentimental glorification of this region, his concern was to show his compatriots "that it's not bad right close by, and that in the Mark Brandenburg, too, one finds historic cities, old castles, beautiful lakes, unique landscape features and excellent fellows wherever one goes."

Visitors to Brandenburg who want to see some culture must decide which of the many castles and manor houses they want to see. Yet, Sanssouci must be on the list. Whoever gets the chance should listen to Johann Sebastian Bach's Brandenburg Concertos in the authentic surroundings of a splendid palace hall – an exceptional experience!

Christian churches have been built in Brandenburg for about one thousand years. Christianity took root in Brandenburg about the year 950 and displaced three-headed Triglaw and the other gods of the Sorbs and Wends. The Slavic minority in Lower Lusatia originally came from the Balkan region. In Brandenburg and Upper Lusatia in Saxony, the Sorbs and Wends have been able to preserve their cultural identity and their own language.

There are more than 1,500 churches in the march; even in tiny villages, we find surprisingly large houses of worship. Many are badly in need of repair; those that have been restored testify to a deeply rooted faith. The medieval monasteries of Lehnin and Chorin are outstanding, to mention only two of the sixteen former Cistercian abbeys. Today, Lehnin houses welfare and social work institutions; Chorin – once a magnificent complex – is a restored semi-ruin that breathes the essence of a lost age. Musical performances in the former church, this showpiece of the march's Gothic brick architecture, leave behind a lasting impression. The Catholic monastery church of St. Mary in Neuzelle is something unique in mainly Protestant Brandenburg. Originally built in the Gothic style, it was transformed to Baroque in the 17th and 18th centuries. Its opulent décor stands up to comparison with any Baroque church of Bavaria or Austria.

Visits to the concentration camp memorials are a chilling experience. Sachsenhausen concentration camp near Oranienburg was built in 1936. Until the end of Nazi rule, approximately 100,000 people were murdered there and in the many external camps. Over 90,000 women and children perished in the Ravensbrück women's camp near Fürstenberg, set up in 1938. Some of these sites were used after the war by the Soviet occupying forces, to intern people they believed did not fit in with the new – Stalinist – system.

The Red Army occupied the march in spring of 1945. Many Brandenburg cities were destroyed especially at the end of the Second World War. The story of the ignominious end of the "Third Reich" and the reorganization of Europe is told by Cecilien-

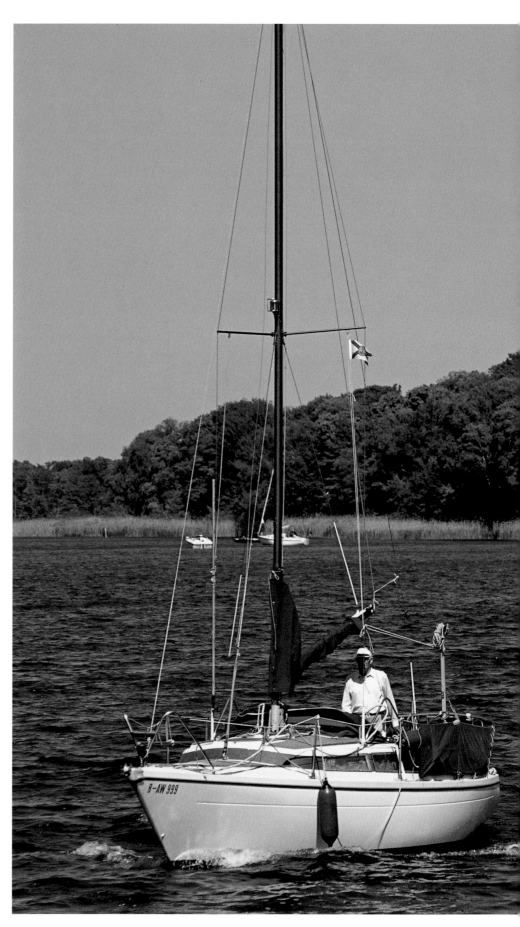

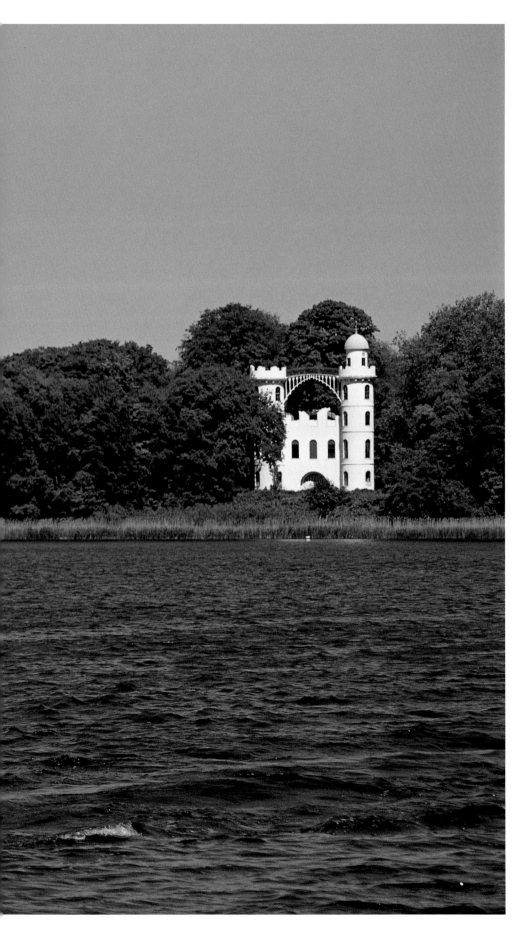

Pfaueninsel (Peacock Island) situated near Wannsee in the Havel, is a nature reserve. In 1793, the Prussian King Frederick William II purchased it and set up a menagerie and a zoo there.

hof Palace, where history was written with the "Potsdam Conference." The heads of state of the USA, the Soviet Union and Great Britain, Truman, Stalin and Churchill – later Attlee –, negotiated the future of Germany here.

After dissolution of the state of Prussia by the Allies in 1947, the province of Mark Brandenburg became a Land. In 1949, Brandenburg became part of the German Democratic Republic (East Germany) founded 7 October. The following year, the prime ministers of East Germany and Poland declared the Oder and Neisse rivers the national border. Upon the administrative reform of 1952, Brandenburg was divided up into the districts of Potsdam, Frankfurt (Oder) and Cottbus.

The old towns of the march accommodate architectural gems, art treasures and other cultural goods. By contrast, Eisenhüttenstadt has little to offer of such things; the town on the Polish border was created on the drawing board in the 1950s as accommodation for the workers of the ironworks combine. Walter Ulbricht himself was involved in the blueprints for the "first Socialist city on German soil," replacing the planned towering high rises with broad, low structures. There is no better place for the documentary centre "Everyday Culture in the GDR" than Eisenhüttenstadt, which was called Stalinstadt from 1953 to 1961.

Twenty kilometres (12 miles) northeast of Berlin, in the Wandlitz forest neighbourhood, we can view the houses – from the outside only – in which the members of the politburo and the leaders of the GDR, such as Grotewohl, Ulbricht, Mielke and Honecker, lived. The dreary 1950s architecture, situated in a nature preserve, is today used by a clinic. Babelsberg Filmpark presents another cultural aspect of the recent past and the present. In the days of silent movies, many a star of the silver screen stood before the camera in this legendary filmmaking town. Visitors can look behind the scenes and see props and characters from famous films and television series.

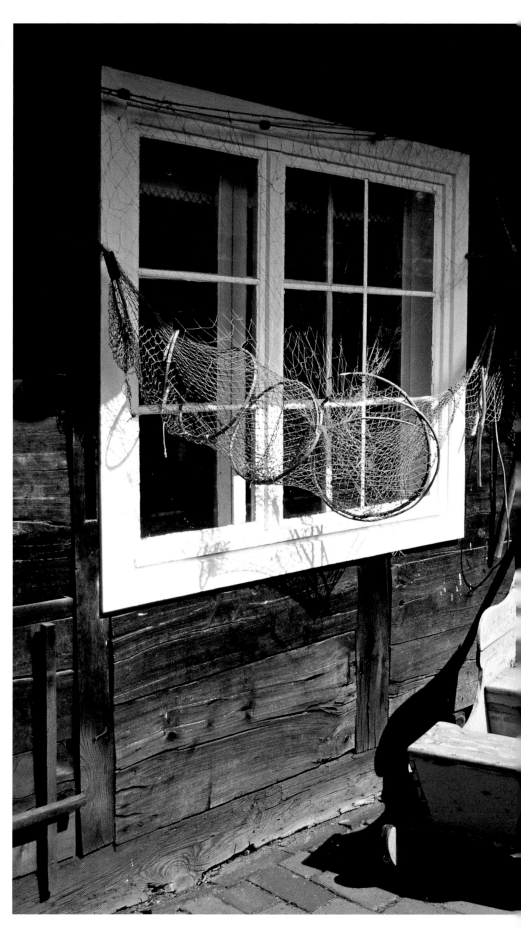

Wünsdorf, the "town of books and bunkers" to the south of Berlin, has transformed itself from a military town to a cultural site. At one time, Wünsdorf was the most strategically important site of the Warsaw Pact in Central Europe. Here, in 1968, the invasion of Czechoslovakia was masterminded. The garrisons have moved out and been replaced by antiquarian booksellers, historians and artists. Bookworms can spend hours browsing the hundreds of thousands of books here.

The engineering feats of lignite mining are both fascinating and terrifying: near Cottbus, gigantic diggers gnaw away at the earth and shovel up the brown gold. Hundreds of villages had to be abandoned for it, roads and rivers were rerouted. Left behind were dismal, cratered, moonlike landscapes. Lignite mining on the eastern edge of the city will be completed in 2010; the hollow will be flooded to create the largest artificial lake in Lusatia.

BRANDENBURG'S WATER WORLDS

With 3,000 lakes, Brandenburg is the most "watery" state in Germany. If you are not up for a swim, you can sit quietly on a reed-lined shore in the company of the swans or watch as a stork majestically rises into the air. With so many waters, angler's need not wait long for an eel, pikeperch or carp to bite.

Yet, not only nature lovers get their due: in Niederfinow there is an elevator for ships. This engineering marvel made the rivers Havel and Oder navigable. The first stage consists of more than a dozen sluices. Construction of the imposing 112-metre (368-foot) long and 33-metre (108-foot) wide ship lift began in 1927. Since 1934, ships can overcome a height of 36 metres (118 feet) in only five minutes in an 85-metre (280-foot) long caisson; the lift moves 4,300 tonnes.

The rivers Spree, Havel, Rhin, Nuthe and Dahme make up 33,000 kilometres (20,500 miles) of flowing water plus streams and

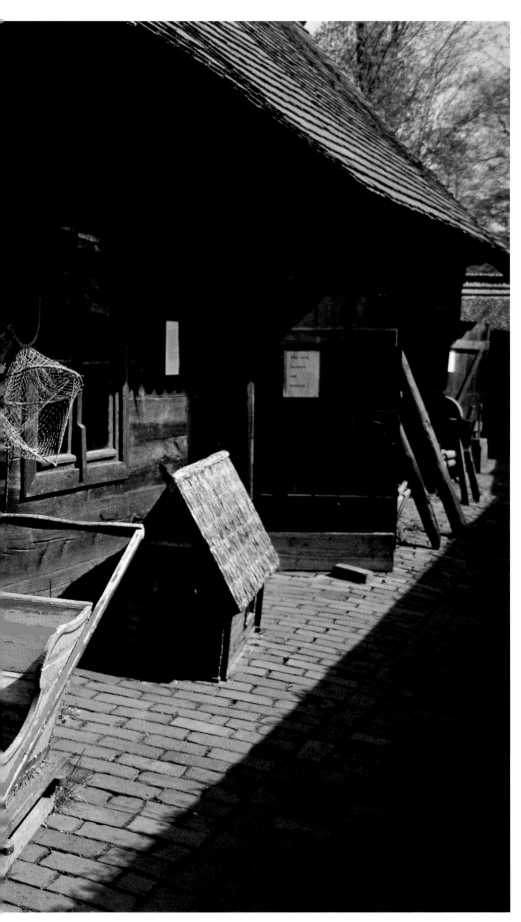

canals; 8,000 kilometres (5,000 miles) can be navigated by paddleboat and 1,600 (995 miles) by motorboat. A trip by punt through the Spreewald is far more leisurely. Some landscapes of Brandenburg, such as the Oderbruch and the Spreewald, are under nature conservation. Yet broad stretches of the march can only be described as barren, the monotony broken only by an occasional tree-lined avenue.

Nevertheless, everything is good for something, as the Brandenburg expert Werner Schumann once wrote: "The secluded and enigmatic march landscape – how it dampened any arrogance, as it raised generations of people to simplicity, straightforwardness and reliability, to that quiet, good-natured, self-confident pride that avoids hasty decisions and stands loyally by the given word."

TRIUMPH OF A TUBER

Brandenburg's traditional cuisine seems just as modest. The main staple is the potato, which began its triumphant advance through German lands from here. It was Frederick William I, the father of Frederick the Great, who decreed by law that the tubers be planted. The first potatoes in the march were planted in 1739 in Hohenfinow. The farmers mistrusted the plants, which matured invisibly underground, fearing that consuming them would cause stupidity. The king could not have known that the potato was planted in South America as early as the 2nd century AD, but he did know that the tuber would be able to sate the hunger of his people. He threatened to cut the noses and ears off farmers who refused to grow potatoes. It is also said that he had potato fields guarded by soldiers to incite curiosity. In the early years, therefore, planting and consumption had to be ordered; later Frederick the Great consistently pursued this policy. After the Seven Years' War, the potato saved the suffering population from starvation.

Another historic decision influenced the development of Brandenburg's cuisine as well: the Edict of Potsdam, which permitted Huguenots to settle in Brandenburg. They brought their recipes with them among their other belongings. Before their arrival to the march, fresh vegetables were a rarity on the tables. Today, potatoes and vegetables are the staples of all meals. *Pomme de terre* are prepared in every possible variation; potato soup is especially recommendable. Strangely enough, in the Uckermark, potatoes are called "noodles."

The white turnips that grow well in the sandy soils of the march were famous; the poet Goethe once had the so-called "Teltower Rübchen" delivered to Weimar via mail coach and even Napoleon appreciated their fine flavour. Spreewald horseradish and gherkins are popular far beyond Brandenburg. One regional home-cooked dish consists of curd cheese seasoned with milk, caraway, salt and pepper, then spread over potatoes boiled in their skins and all topped with chopped onions and a good dash of linseed oil.

In the old days, fancier foods like fish, which is always fresh in the water-rich march, were served only on Sundays and holidays. Favourite regional fish dishes include pike in Spreewald gravy made of buttermilk and beer, catfish in sour cream, Havel pikeperch in horseradish sauce or marinated green eels.

Your sweet tooth can look forward to *Klemmkuchen*: waffles baked on heavy irons, filled with whipped cream or "Prince Pückler" ice cream – strawberry, vanilla and chocolate – or *Plinsen*: egg pancakes with melted butter, cinnamon and sugar or plum jam.

Some foods, such as Werder fruit wine, are good souvenirs. Typical mementos taken home from the Spreewald are dolls in local costume, wooden clogs, painted Easter eggs or blue dyed tablecloths. Rheinsberg ceramics have a good reputation. Pictorial broadsheets from Neuruppin are extraordinary, once a sort of illustrated magazine with (often imaginary) events of world history and educational or inspirational motifs. Between 1810 and 1937, 100 million copies of 22,000 different motifs are said to have been sold; then and now, people preferred pictures to words. The market for the broadsheets fell through with the rise of magazines, radio and movies. Take an entertaining tour of the exhibition in Neuruppin, where reprints of the broadsheets can be purchased. Ulti-

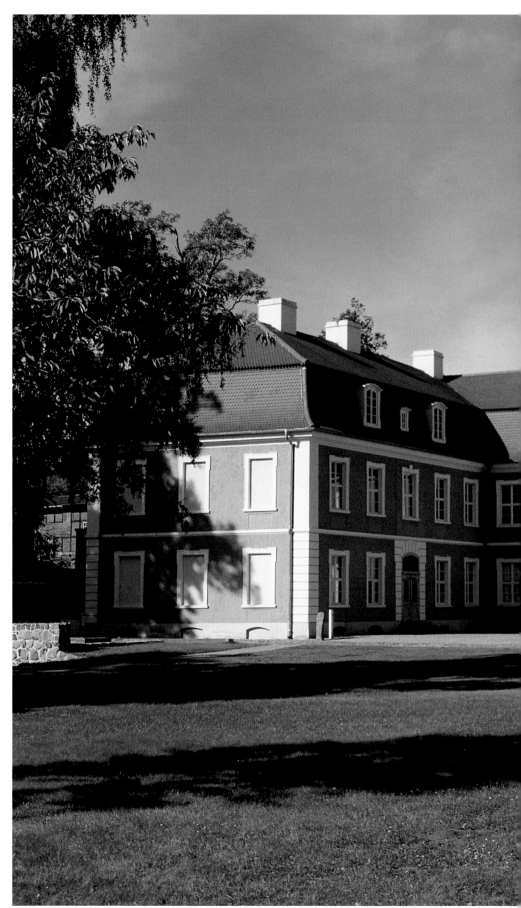

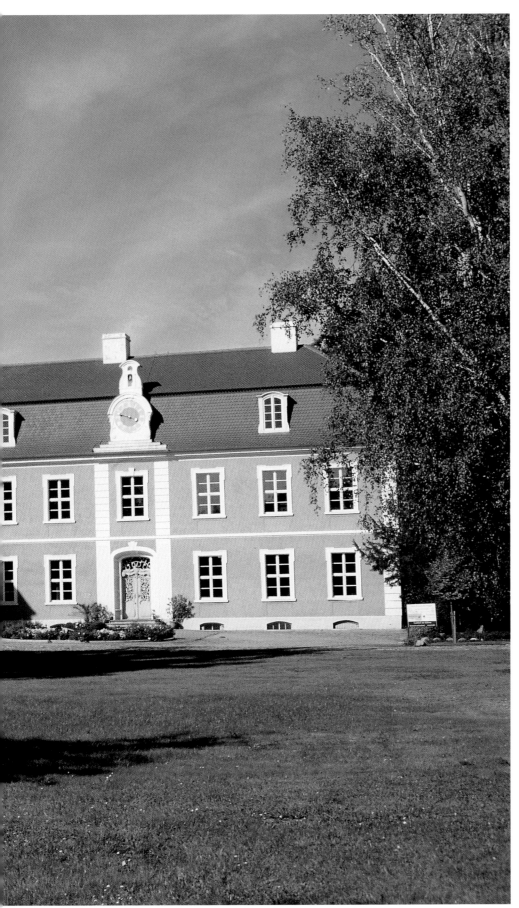

mately, every town tries to market its name somehow on a product label, even if it is merely a coffee mug with the logo "Liebenwalder Kaffeepott." Other souvenirs include books by Fontane and other authors of the march, picture books, calendars and postcards with pictures of Brandenburg, or tapes and CDs with "Music from the Court of Frederick the Great."

"Should you travel, you ask, travel in the Mark?" writes Fontane in his *Rambles*, not without rhetorical finesse. He advocates discovering the terrain that has so much to offer. Yet he offers no simple answer. Fontane warns, "He who wishes to travel in the Mark must first bring along love for the place and people, or at least no prejudice. He must have the good will to see the good in what is good, instead of ruining it with carping comparisons." This still applies today. Fontane says one needs a finer sense for nature and landscapes in order to travel Brandenburg and profit, for those who demand a glacier or a storm-swept sea will not be satisfied. Mark Brandenburg possesses the proverbial "seven beauties." Further, the poet wisely writes, "One merely needs to know how to find them. Those who have eyes for this, dare and travel."

Pages 22/23:
In 1958, Werner Schumann wrote that the Heiligengrabe convent in the Prignitz and the other monasteries in the march are "crumbling monuments, rootless since the 16th century and bereft of real life: mythical witnesses in the weathered golden shimmer of a fading millennium." – Yet today, the 13th century church still has a festive glow. Once the pilgrimage destination for relic-seekers, today the pilgrimage destination of tourists.

Pages 24/25:
The clear water of Lake Zechlin in the Ruppiner Land makes it a favourite with water sport enthusiasts. Rowers, canoeists, sailors and surfers find all they can desire in the waters of Brandenburg.

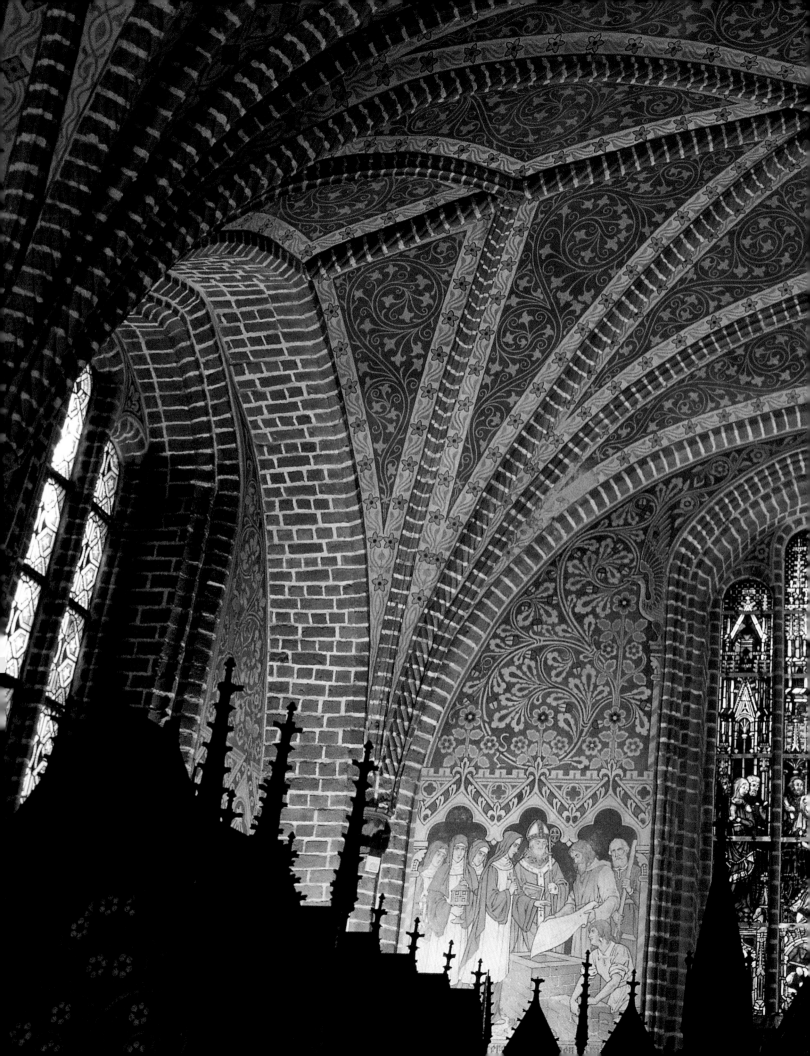

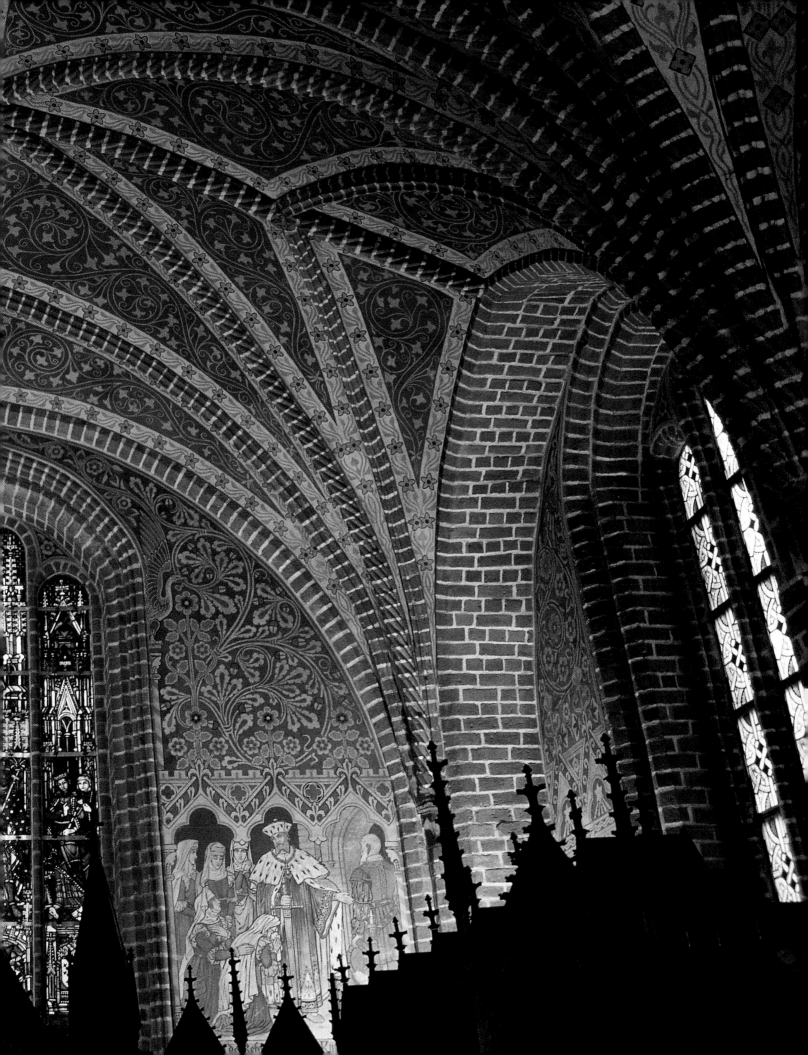

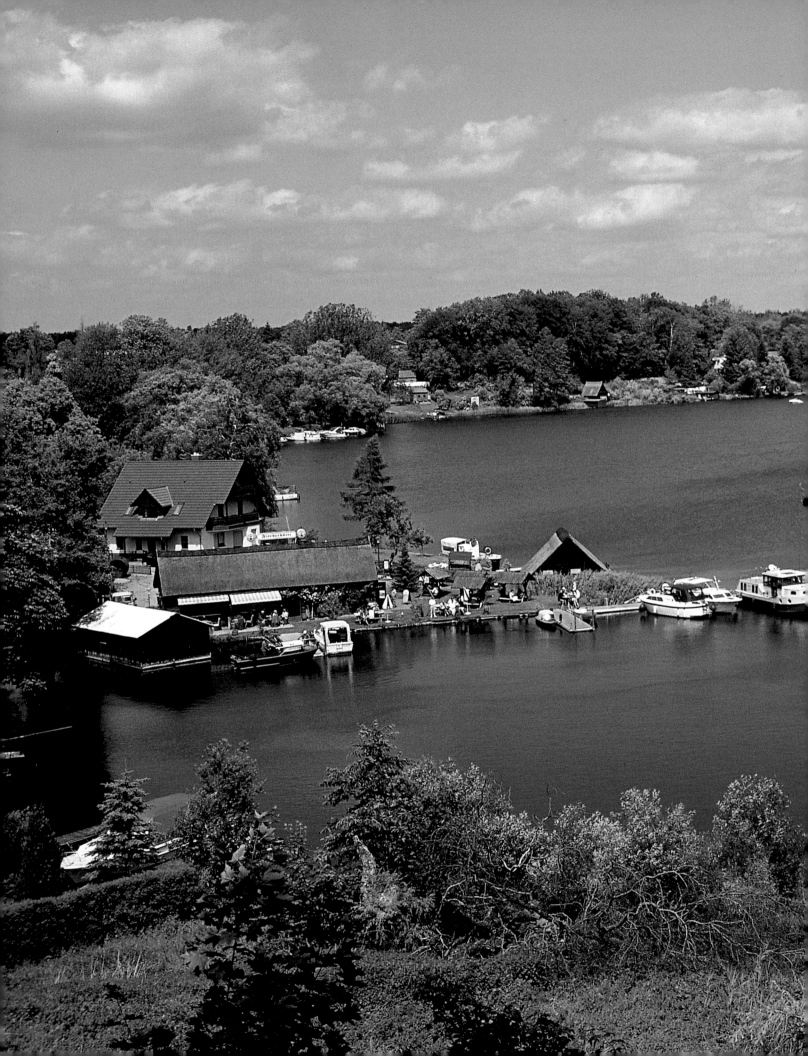

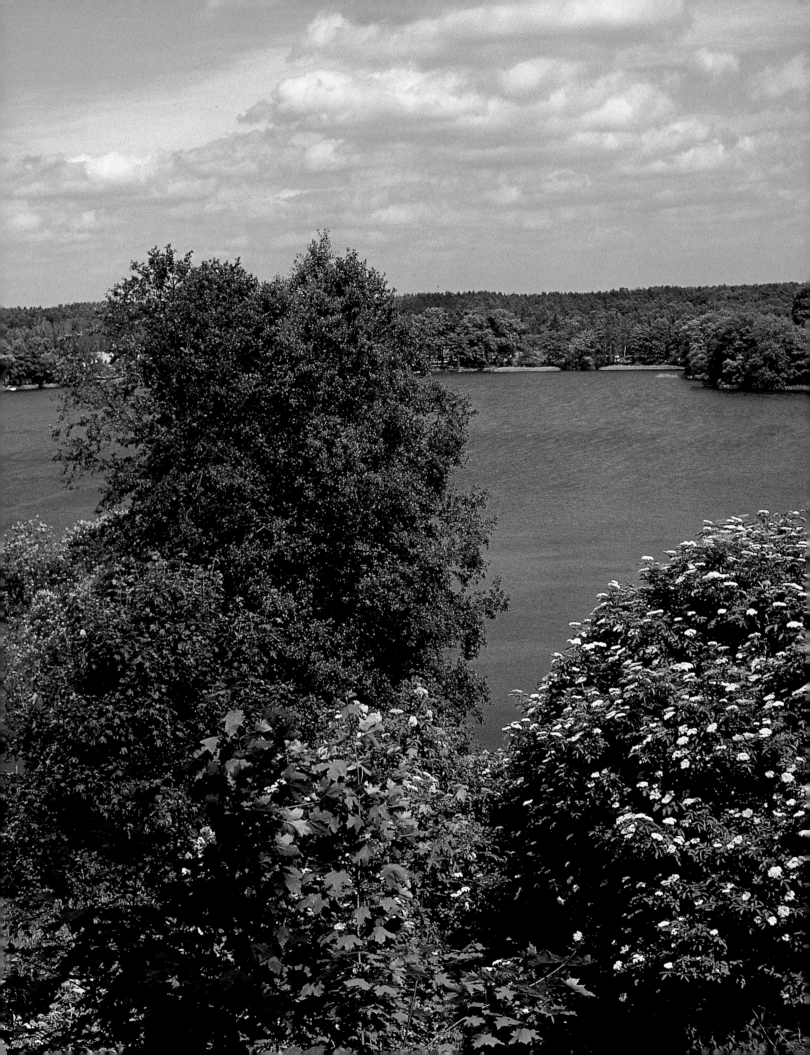

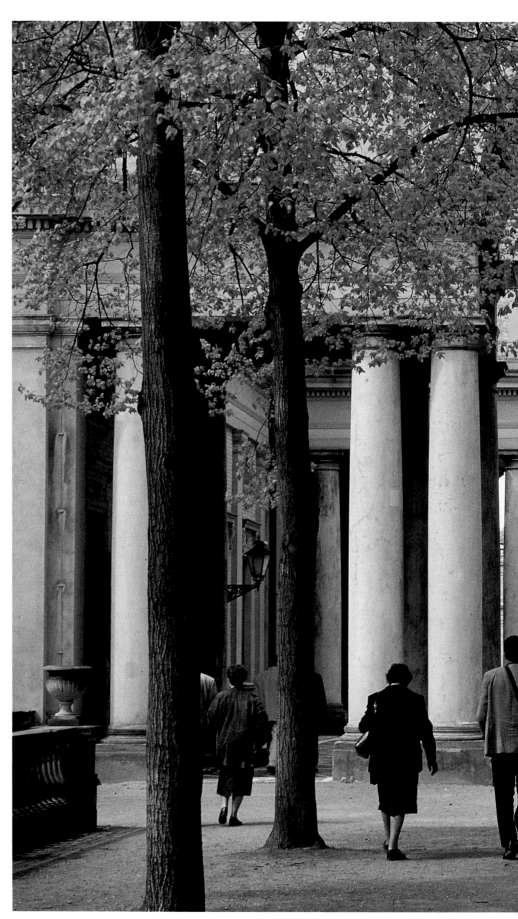

Antique flair in Sanssouci: the pillar gallery leads visitors to the Neue Orangerie, which was constructed between 1851 and 1860 after the ideas of Frederick William IV and the plans of architect Ludwig Persius.

As the royal summer residence, Potsdam, the capital of Brandenburg, has more than its share of sights: above all, the complex at Sanssouci, but Nikolai Church and the Old City Hall as well, the Russian colony with its log cabins and the orthodox Alexander Newski Church, not to mention the red brick Dutch Quarter. The city lost two landmarks: in 1959-60, the remains of the Stadtschloss, badly damaged by bombing the night of 14 April 1945, were cleared away. The Garrison Church was used as a backdrop by Hitler and Hindenburg for their photo-op handshake on 21 March 1933, the "Day of Potsdam." It burned down in 1945 and the surviving tower was demolished in 1968.

The cradle of the state of Brandenburg is the town of the same name situated on a number of islands in the Havel. The Slavic "Brennaburg" was conquered in the 10th century by King Henry I. In 948, a bishopric was founded there. In 1165, the foundation stone was laid for the Cathedral of St. Peter and Paul, one of the state's most important sacred structures.

Other towns are just as remarkable; Ribbeck for instance, which was made famous by Theodor Fontane's ballad: "Squire von Ribbeck at Ribbeck in Havelland, in his garden there stood a pear tree grand…" Havelland and Fläming – named after its Flemish immigrants – contain a few towns with well-preserved historical centres: Werder, the island in the river, the pilgrimage site of Beelitz and Jüterbog, the medieval capital of Fläming.

The state has the highest elevation on the North German Plain, the 201-metre (660-foot) high Hagelberg. It is a revitalizing region – or as Albert Einstein said of Caputh on Lake Schwielow, where he owned a summerhouse, "Come to Caputh; forget the world!"

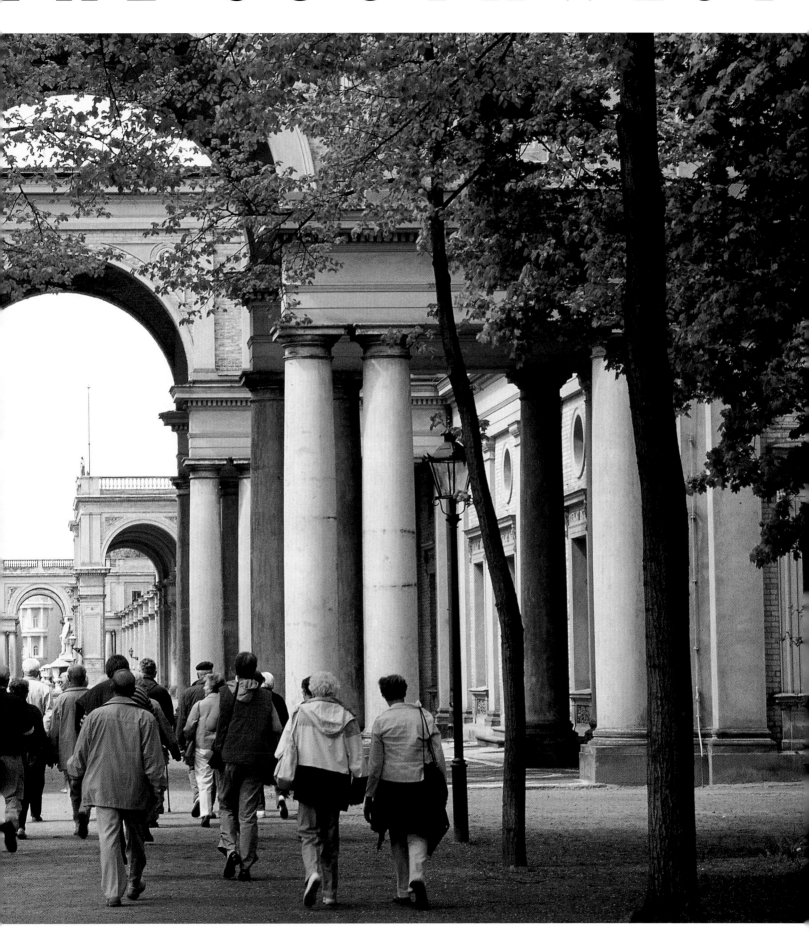

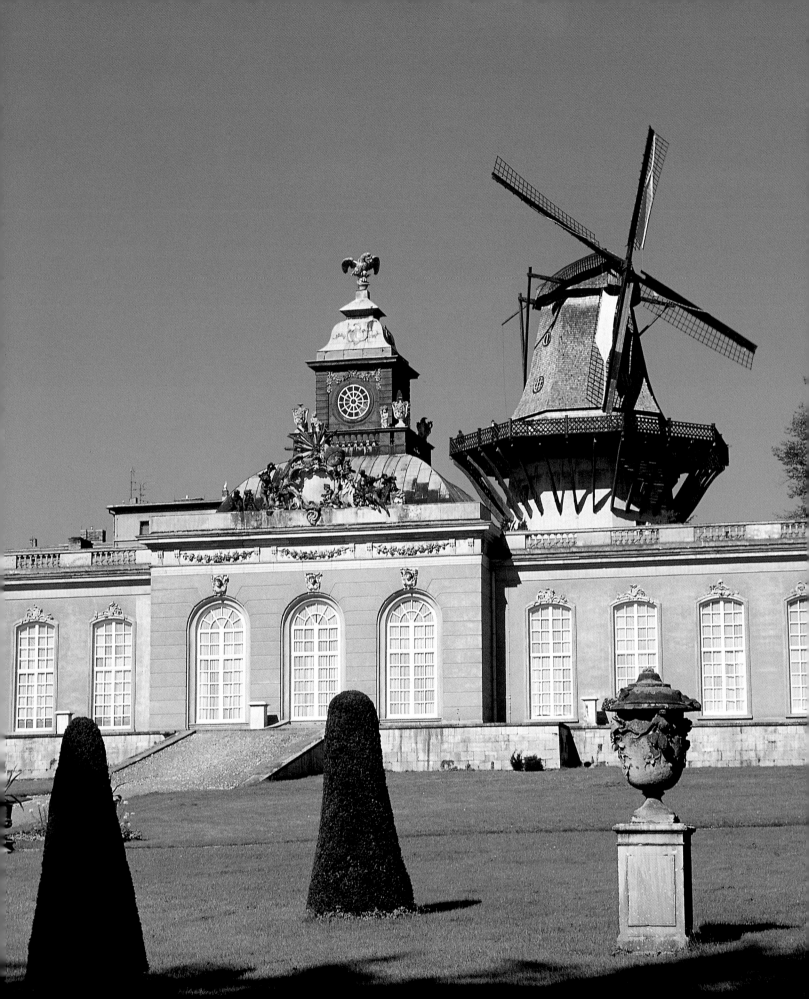

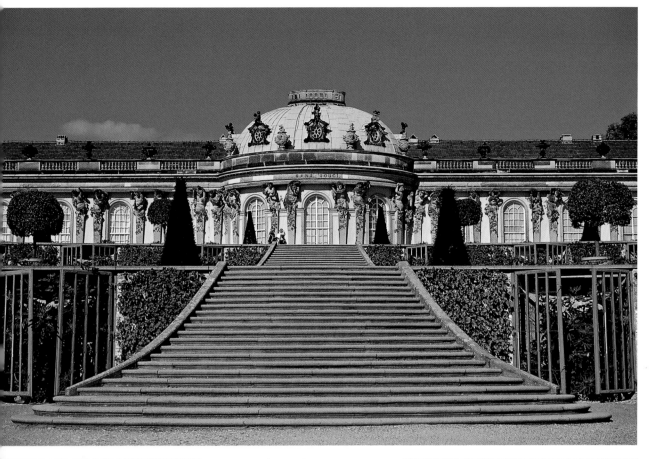

The architects of Sanssouci advised the king to put the stairs closer to the palace so that one could see it even from below and so that the perspective would not "swallow up" a part of it. Still, Frederick won out and demanded a patio wide enough to sit on or stroll with his guests.

Left-hand page:
Built as an orangerie in 1747 by von Knobels-dorff: the New Chambers on the park grounds of Sanssouci. Later it was turned into a guesthouse and rooms for festive occasions, such as the shining Jaspissaal. The historical mill from the 18th century burned down at the end of the war in 1945; it was reconstructed in 1993. From it, visitors can enjoy a lovely view of the grounds.

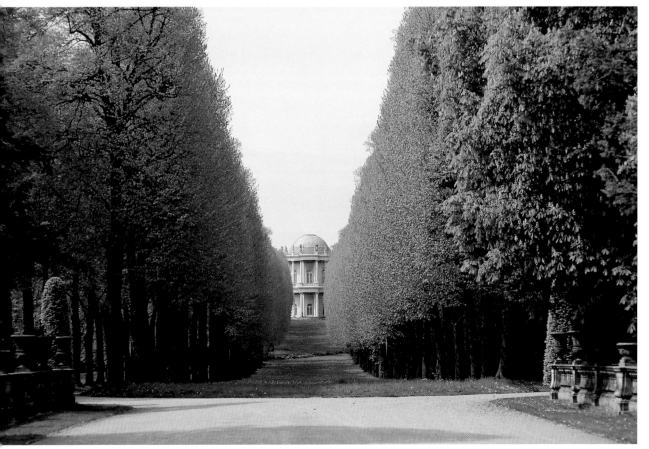

In the park at Sanssouci. The Belvedere is the last structure built on the orders of Frederick the Great himself. It was constructed in the Italian style between 1770 and 1772 according to plans by Georg Christian Unger.

In the palace gardens of Sanssouci, visitors can enjoy the marvellous fountains unlike Old Fritz; the complicated engineering for the waterworks failed after one half hour of operation and never bubbled again in the king's lifetime.

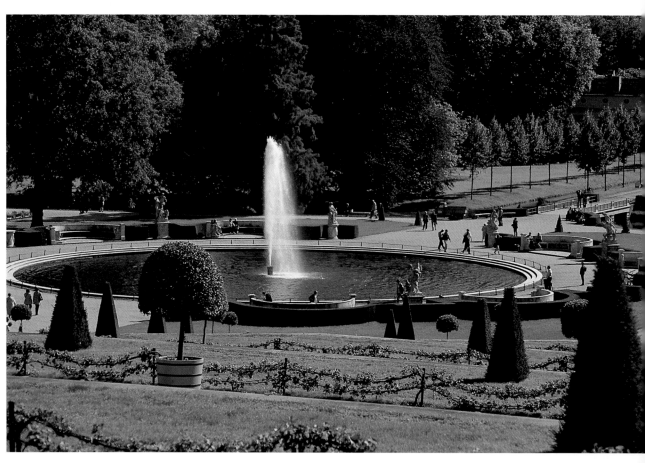

Right-hand page:
A travel description written in the year 1900 states: "The park grounds of Sanssouci are described by all visitors, local and foreign, as grand, and rightly so. They were given their shape chiefly by the great Prussian garden architect Peter Josef Lenné. A kaleidoscope composition of nature, art and history forms a whole, which, in its harmonious overall effect, touches each visitor beneficially and allows them to take their leave fully satisfied."

The magic of the Far East is called up by the decorative Chinese House, erected between 1754 and 1757 on the grounds of Sanssouci. The layout has the shape of a cloverleaf; three chambers arranged about a rotund central hall. It houses fine porcelain from China and Meissen and Chinese silk apparel of the 18th century. Visitors are welcomed by gold-plated figures of Chinese tea sippers.

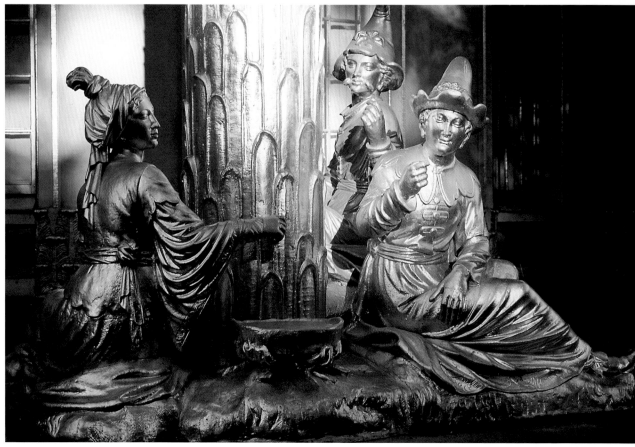

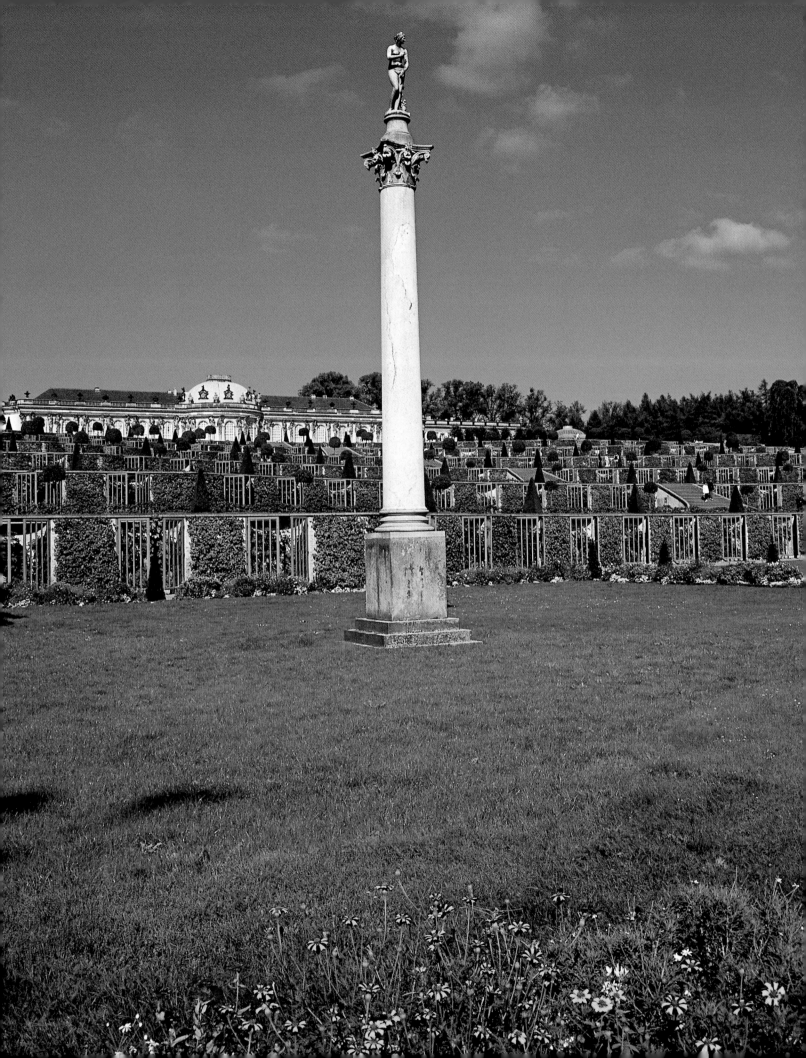

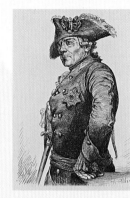

Jean-Jacques Rousseau said of Frederick II: "He thinks like a philosopher, but governs like a king." – This 1859 book illustration is by Adolph von Menzel.

It cannot be compared to Versailles or Schönbrunn in terms of size, but certainly in terms of importance: Sanssouci Palace – "without care" – is a top-notch sight and is under protection as a UNESCO world heritage site. The one-story building – approximately one hundred metres (330 feet) wide and twelve metres (40 feet) high – is rather modest in appearance. The overall impression of the 300-hectare (740-acre) grounds is "care freeing."

This is where Prussia's King Frederick II sought to come closer to nature. He drew the plans for the little palace himself, including the idea of building terraces into the vineyard in front where figs could ripen in niches

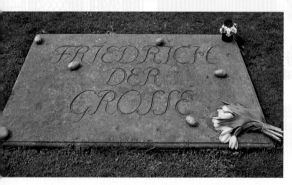

behind glass. His court architect Georg Wenzeslaus von Knobelsdorff executed the work. Landscape architect Peter Joseph Lenné laid out the marvellous gardens.

In utopian Sanssouci, we can imagine the aesthete Frederick writing poems, holding flute recitals, meeting with Johann Sebastian Bach or philosophizing with Voltaire. Born in 1712, the prince attempted to flee the strict upbringing of his father, "soldier king" Frederick I. His punishment was two years incarceration. After their reconciliation, Frederick led an artist's life in castle Rheinsberg, but after the death of his father in 1740, the crown and rule passed to him. To the as-

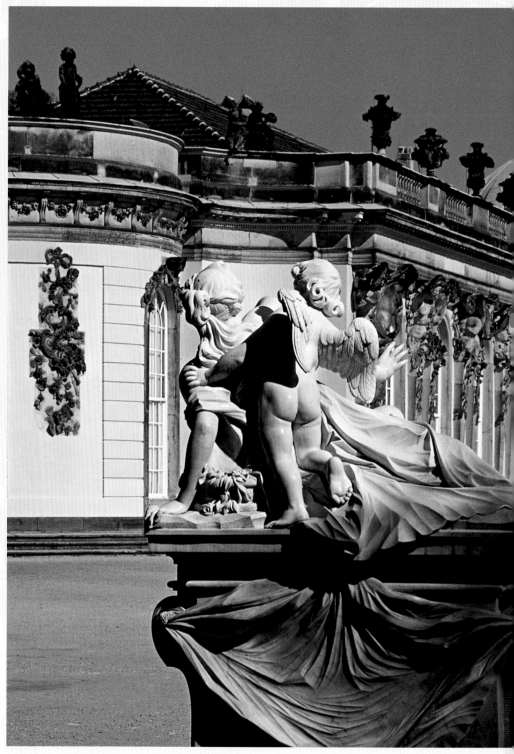

Left:
"With every passing day I lose some of my vital force and peu à peu approach the dwelling from whence no one has yet sent a message," wrote Frederick to Voltaire in 1773. In death, he had to endure an odyssey before finally reaching his final resting place in this simple tomb.

Above:
"Sans, souci" boasts the façade – this unusual spelling provokes speculation even today: "without," Frederick would have probably had even more worry.

Above righ
Originally, the kin sought intimacy an simplicity in his summe residence outside Berli Over time, the comple grew to eight hundre hectare

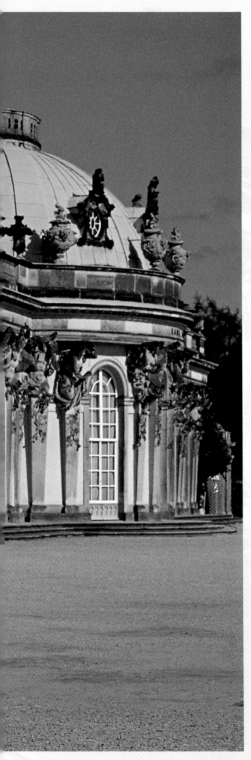

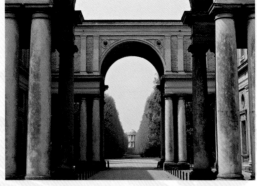

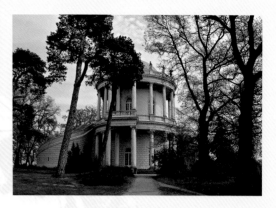

tonishment of Europe, he suddenly instigated wars, such as the Silesian and Seven Years' War. During his reign, his subjects doubled in number to approximately eleven million; he expanded his dominions at the cost of Poland and Austria from 120,000 to 200,000 square kilometres (from 47,000 to 77,000 square miles). He has gone down in history as "the Great," an enlightened reformer who considered himself the "first servant of his state." He abolished torture, granted asylum to protestant Huguenots and tolerance to Catholics, created a strong class of civil servants and had free seed potatoes distributed – yet, like this father before him, had to force the peasants to grow them on threat of punishment.

THE FIRST MUSEUM

Parallel to his duties of state, he oversaw Sanssouci, beginning construction in 1745. After completion of the palace, he had an ornamental Baroque garden laid out with 3,000 fruit trees and greenhouses for oranges, melons, peaches and bananas. Following the Seven Years' War (1756–1763), he commissioned the Neue Palais, a two-hundred-room complex, with a façade adorned by 428 figures. The Bildergalerie was completed in 1764. In this first building in Germany to serve solely as a museum, we can still admire masterpieces by Rubens, van Dyck, Tintoretto and Caravaggio today.

As early as 32 years before his death, Frederick decreed in his will that he be buried next to his beloved greyhounds close to the palace. Instead, in 1786 he was buried in the Garrison Church of Potsdam. In 1944, his sarcophagus was moved to St. Elizabeth in Marburg, and in 1952 taken to the family seat, Hohenzollern Castle near Hechingen. Not until 1991 was Frederick's request given its due respect, and he found his final resting place in the vault built during his lifetime next to Sanssouci Palace.

"Old Fritz" is remembered as a multifaceted individual: as a warrior and a poet; as a Prussian king who spoke French whenever possible; as a sensitive and subtle statesman who was skilled in diplomacy but would not tolerate the presence of women around him. He died, solitary, small and stooped, in his beloved Sanssouci, this gem of Frederickan Rococo, a "poem in stone and glass."

Frederick the Second's successors realized their own ideals of beauty on the palace grounds in the form of villas and baths in the Roman style or the Friedenskirche, which emulates ancient basilicas. They would not have pleased the enlightened "philosopher of Sanssouci" as Frederick II called himself in letters to Voltaire – yet his motto was "live and let live."

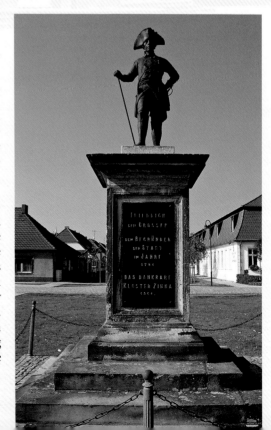

Above far right:
The name of this lovely Roman-style structure means "beautiful view": Belvedere on the Klausberg

Right:
Feared and honoured by his people: many statues once testified to the Prussian peoples' devotion to their king. This one stands in Zinna Monastery.

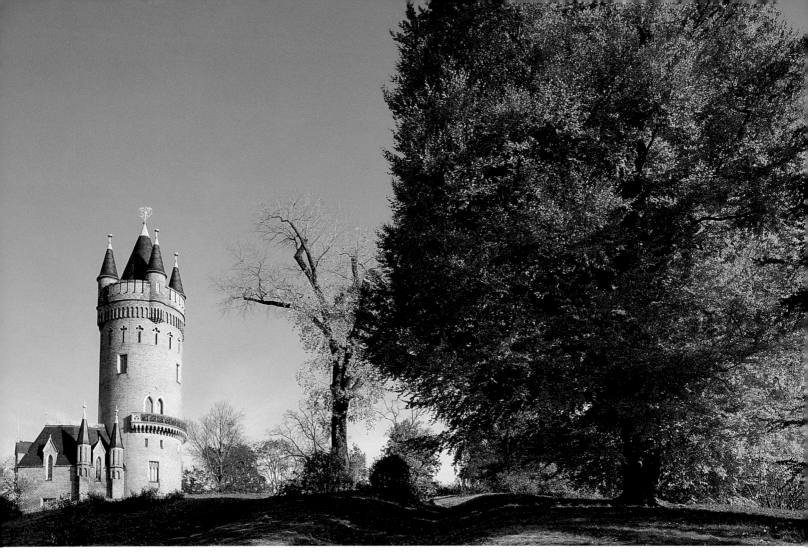

Above:
Similarities with Eschenheim Gate in Frankfurt/Main are not coincidental: it stood model for the Flatow Tower in Potsdam.

Right:
Potsdam's people enjoying pleasant hours at the Moorlake inn. But, what is a "Potsdamer"? A programme on GDR Radio once stated, "There never actually was a pure Potsdamer. He is an adventurous blend of all the peoples of Europe, for who all did not live, love and leave behind children here on the shores of the Havel?"

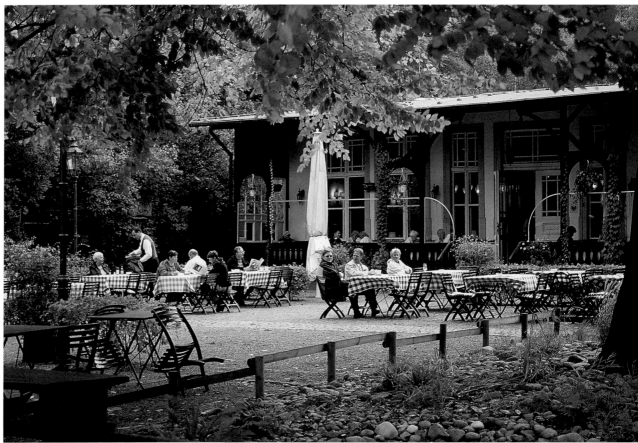

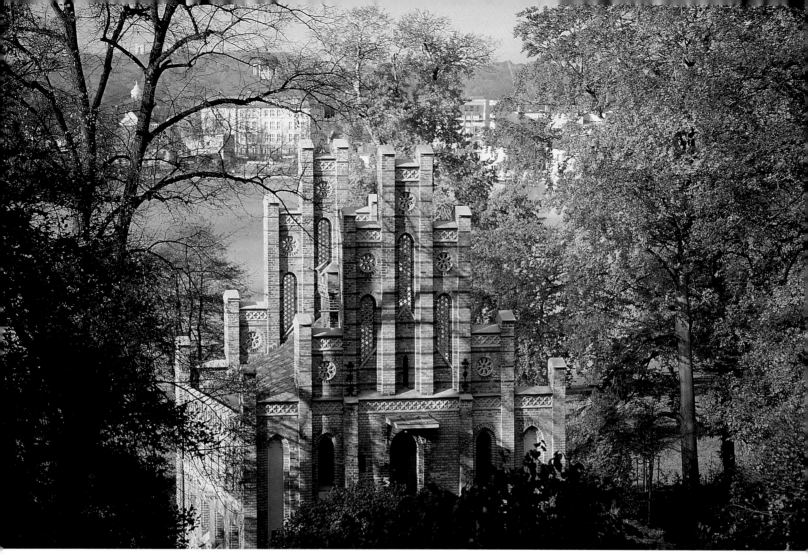

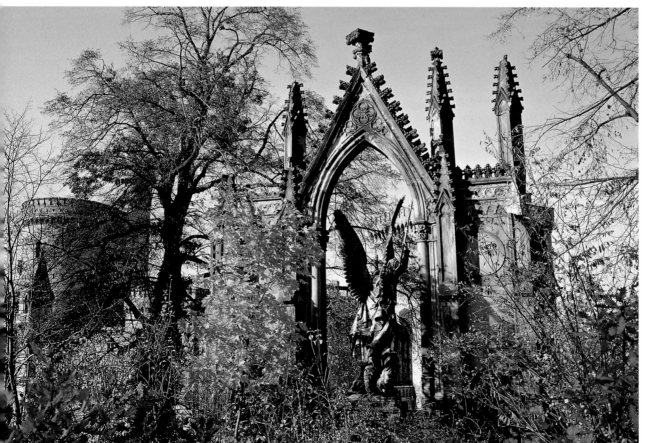

Above:
The sailors' house in Babelsberg Park was built in 1842 in the Neo-Gothic style. The gable was modelled on the Medieval town hall of Stendal.

Left:
Architect Schinkel became inspired by a journey to England, resulting in the Tudor castle he erected between 1833 and 1849 in Babelsberg with its battlements and bay windows. This fountain basin with the archangel Michael stands behind the castle.

The legendary bridge at Glienicke. A bridge has stood on this spot since the 16th century to connect Potsdam and Berlin. The present steel struc- ture dates from 1907. Destroyed in 1945 and reconstructed in 1949, it became a symbol of the separation of east from west. The white borderline between East Germany and West Berlin ran right through its centre. For forty years, it was used as a place to exchange or buy the freedom of top agents or important prisoners. Since reunification, it has been reopened and is the loveliest way to arrive in Potsdam.

Like a ship at anchor, the Church of the Saviour lies on a peninsula in the Jungfern Lake south of Sacrow. Frederick William IV liked to have himself rowed to house of worship dat from 1844, wh decorative arcade arc imitate sacred buildir in Lombar

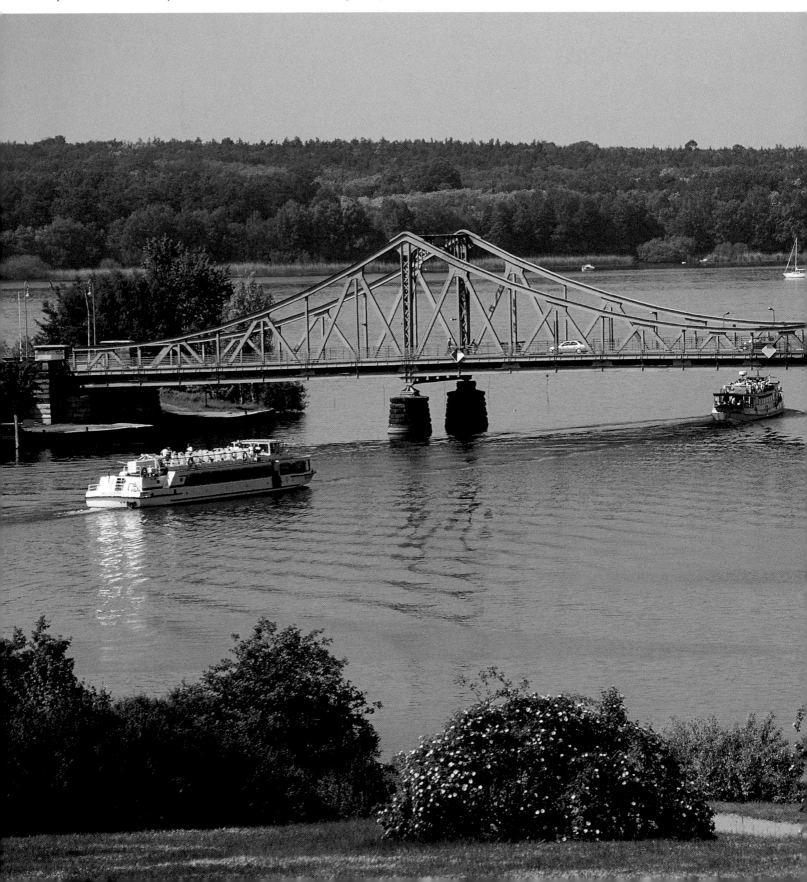

Centre right and below: *A journey through Brandenburg by car is not enough. Only from the water can you have unusual views of landscapes, cities and magnificent churches and palaces. A tour on a passenger ship puts the beauty of the Havelland in the proper perspective. Even centuries ago, boating trips were among the popular pleasures of Brandenburg visitors.*

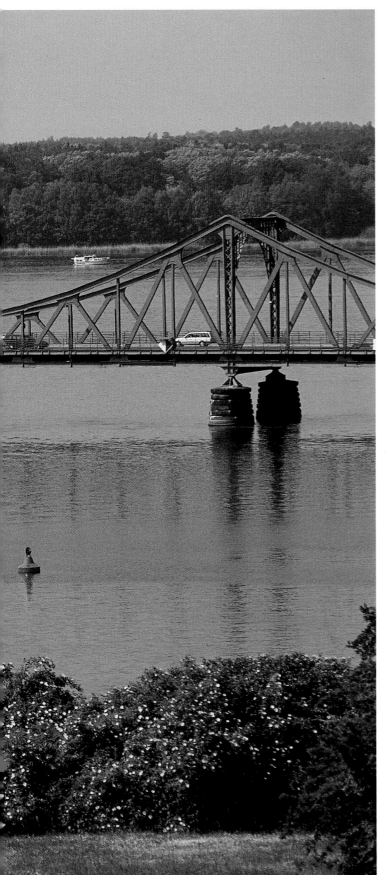

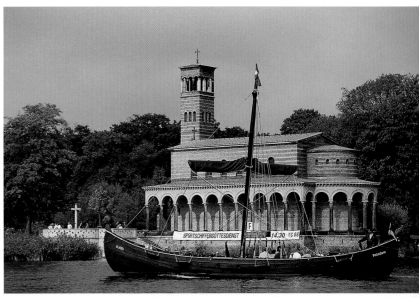

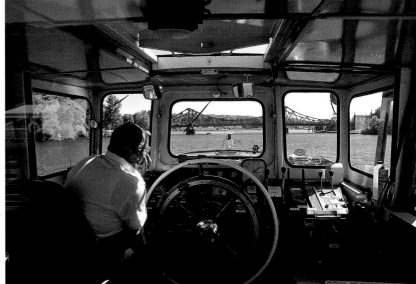

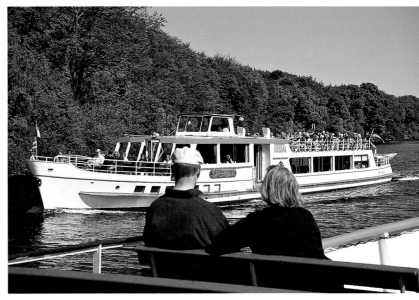

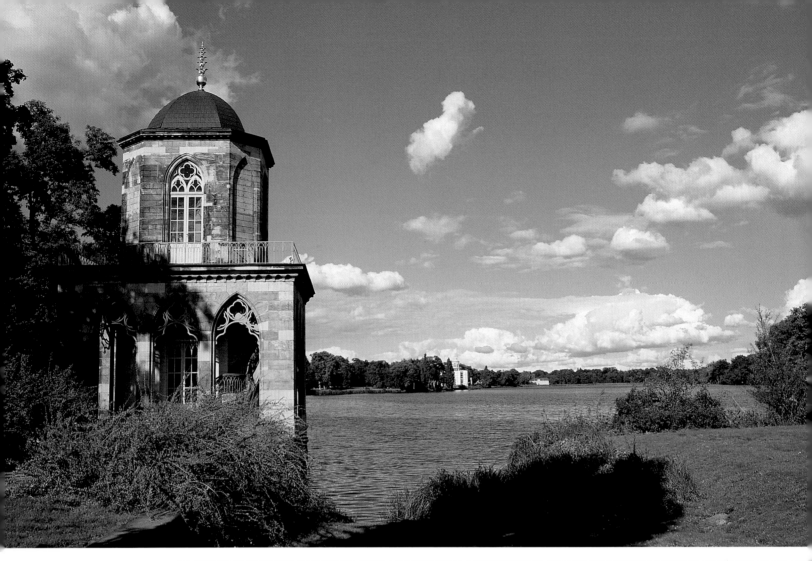

Above:

At the southern end of the New Garden, Frederick William II had his Gothic Library built, a two-story pavilion with a lovely view of the Holy Lake. For half a century, the building was allowed to fall to ruin until, in 1993, it was rebuilt as a gift of the City of Berlin for Potsdam's 1,000-year celebration.

Right:

The Kleine Schloss in the gardens of Babelsberg, erected between 1840 and 1842 in the then-fashionable English Tudor style. This is where Crown Prince Frederick William spent his youth; later it housed the many court ladies, for which it got its by-name Ladies' or Cavaliers' House.

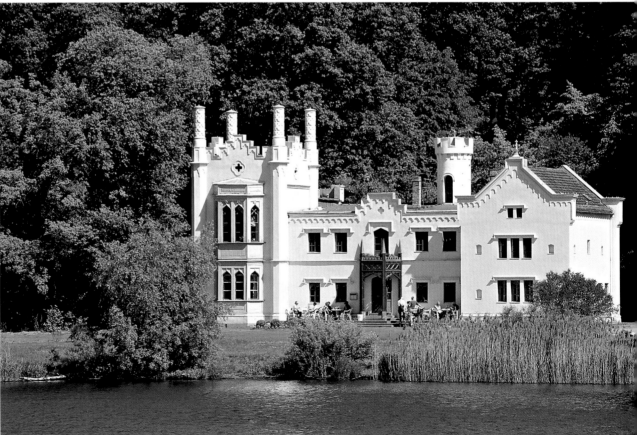

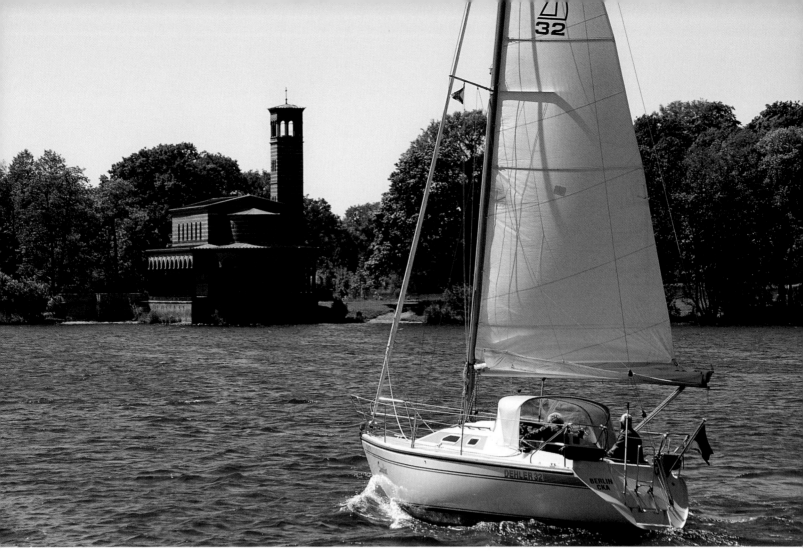

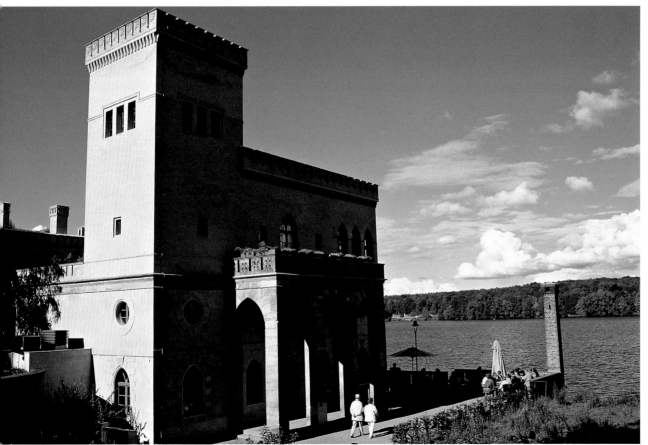

Above:
Like greetings from Italy:
The Church of the
Saviour near Sacrow,
situated picturesquely on
the Havel, built in the
style of an Italian basil-
ica. During the separa-
tion of Germany, it lay
in the death strip and its
campanile was part of
the wall. It was lavishly
restored in the 1990s.

Left:
The cityscape of Potsdam
is characterized by the
Havel. The many river
branches and curves
reveal surprising, lovely
perspectives.

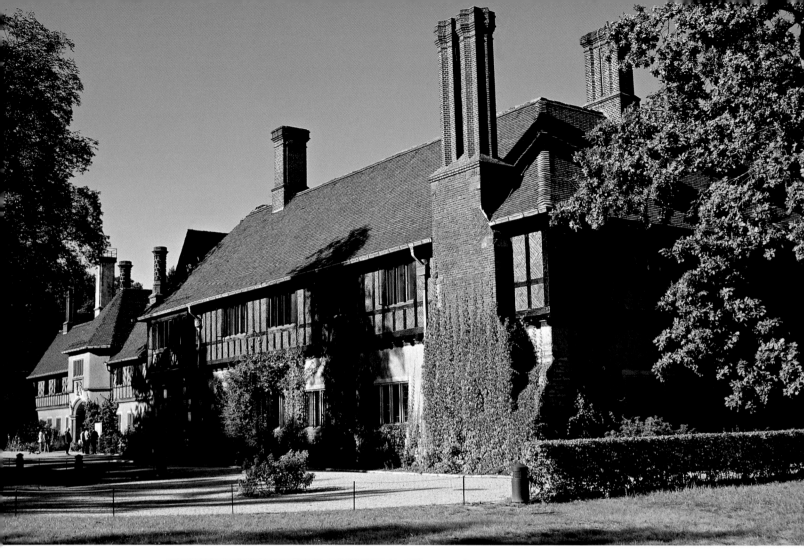

Above:
Cecilienhof, the youngest palace in Prussian history, was completed in 1917 in the style of an English manor house. Crown Prince William of Prussia resided here with his wife Cecilie. World history was written in these rooms when the Potsdam Conference met here from 17 July to 2 August 1945: the victorious powers of the Second World War consulted and decided the fate of the future of Germany. The hall in which Churchill, Truman and Stalin signed the treaty has been preserved as it was on that day.

Right:
A bronze Narcissus admires his reflection in pool in the inner courtyard of Cecilienhof Palace.

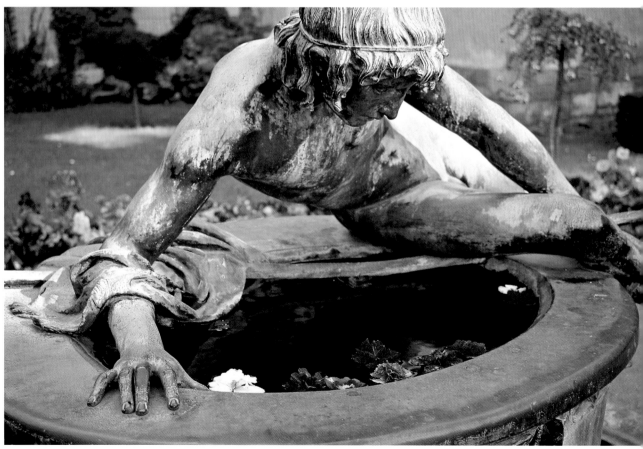

40

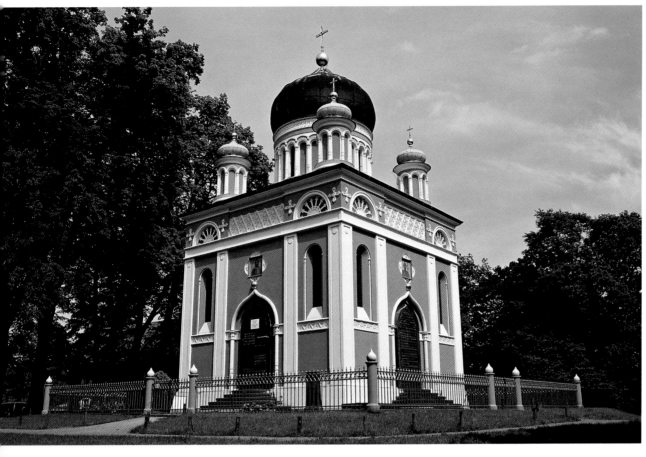

Alexandrowka is the Russian colony in the north of Potsdam. Its church, a square cruciform domed structure is dedicated to Saint Alexander Newski (1220–1263). A pope supervises the church and the small Russian congregation of Potsdam.

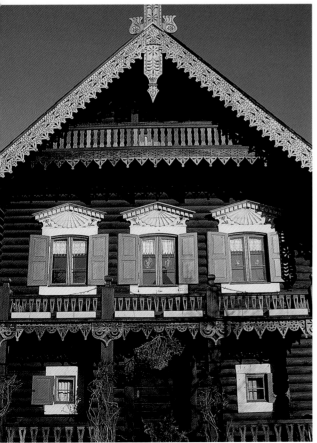

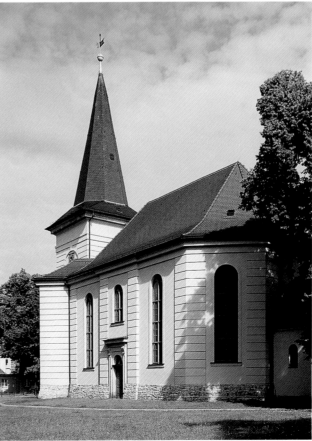

Far left:
The Russian settlement of Alexandrowka was founded in 1826 in Potsdam for Russian choir singers brought to Prussia by Napoleon's campaign. Peter Joseph Lenné built it modelled on Russian soldiers' villages: a bit of home in a foreign place.

Left:
Friedrichskirche on the triangular Weberplatz, the centre of the old weaving colony of Nowawes, today part of Potsdam. It was erected in 1752 by Boumann, the architect of the Dutch Quarter.

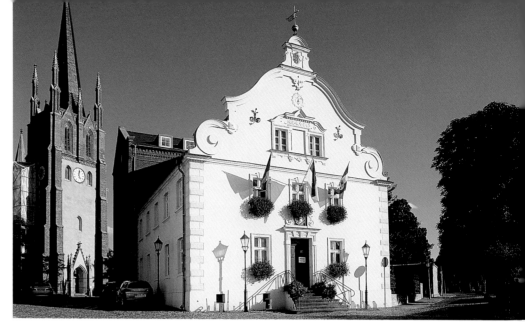

Below:
The historian Ferdinand Ludwig Schönemann was effusive about the green isle of Werder in a book dating from 1784: "In the summertime, when the water is low, one can walk the shores of the island in one hour; to encircle it by boat, whether in a punt or a barge, requires two hours." – Today, a boat trip around the island is still a pleasure.

Right:
Werder, the island in the Havel, was once the orchard of Mark Brandenburg and the brick kiln of Berlin: fruit and bricks made the town famous throughout the country. Its importance is also testified to by the fact that King Frederick William IV personally designed the sketch for the Neo-Gothic Holy Spirit Church built in 1857/1858. Beside it stands the town hall.

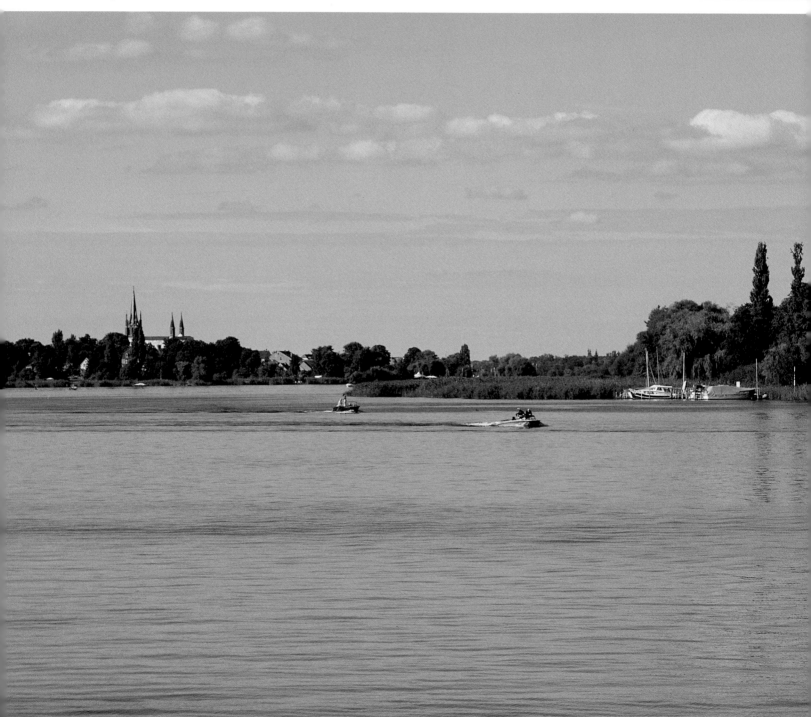

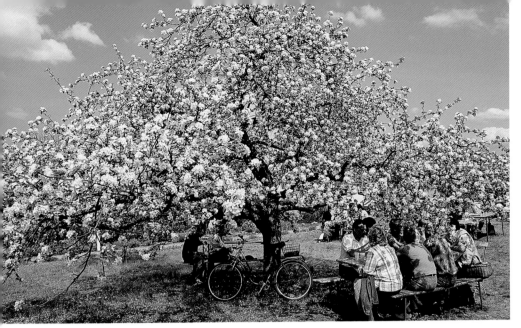

Left:
Wine was once pressed in Werder! Later, the town became famous for its fruit wines. "The currant wine has got a punch," noted the poet Klabund, "everyone cheers and shouts, and sways like the white junks on the Havel." – When the fruit trees blossom, a festival is held; visitors are invited to the orchards to taste the wares.

Centre and below:
Those who live in the middle of the river, live from the river. Werder once was a major fishing town. Although fishing no longer plays an economic role, you can still have freshly caught fish served to you in the rustic ambience of the island's guesthouses – prepared, of course, a la march.

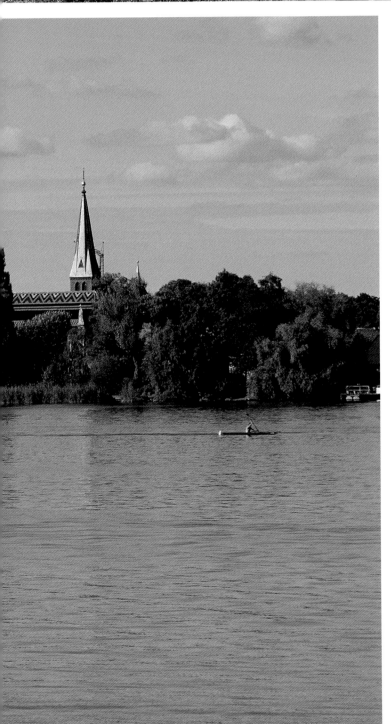

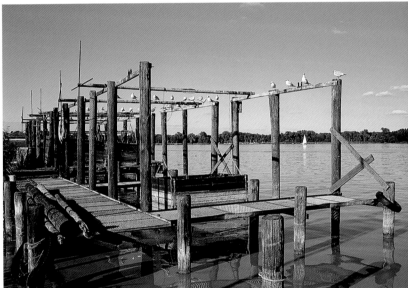

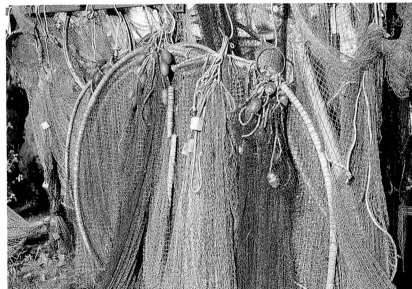

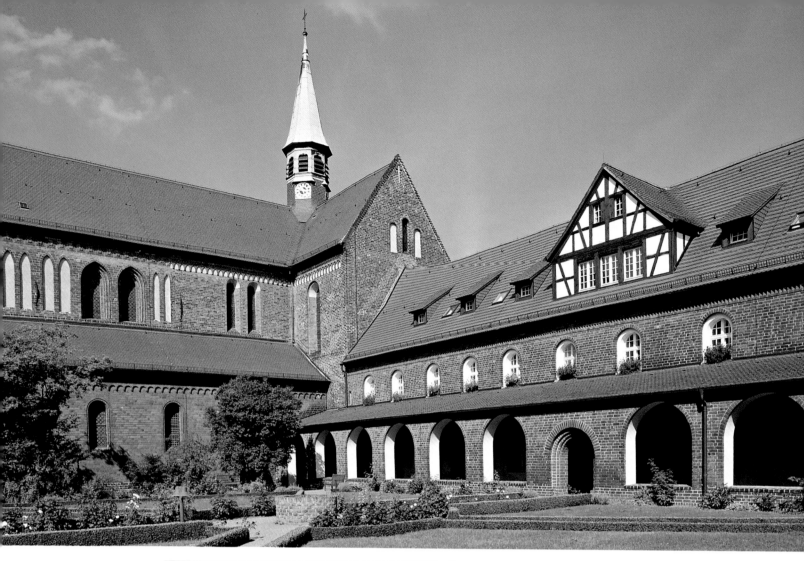

Above:
From 1180 to 1542, monks lived at Lehnin Monastery, then it became the hunting lodge of Elector Frederick William, to finally fall to ruin and use as a quarry. It was restored in the 19th century; since then the Evangelical Lutheran Church operates a deaconess house there with social facilities such as a clinic, nursing homes and children's day care.

Right:
The village church in Staffelde, a Late Gothic brick structure, is usually only open on the weekend. If you want to view it on a weekday – as in many towns here – you can get a key from the neighbours.

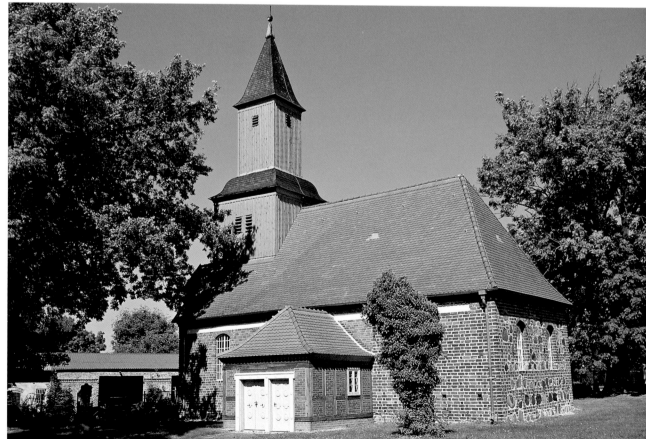

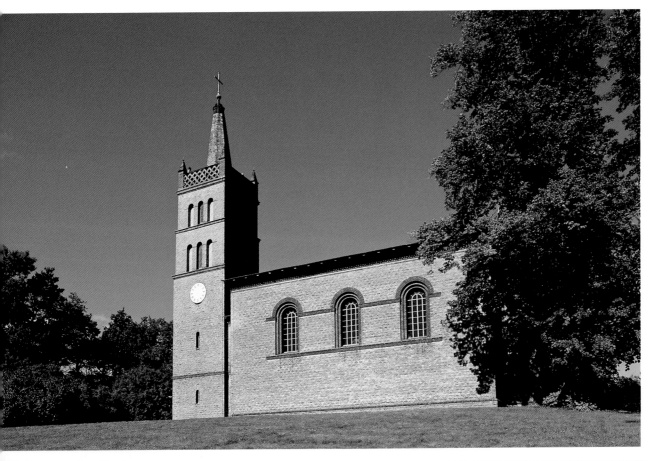

Left:
*From the steeple of the
Protestant church in
Petzow, designed by
Schinkel, you can view
the palace gardens,
designed by landscape
architect Peter Joseph
Lenné, as well as Lake
Schwielow.*

Below:
*The light-flooded
Schinkel church on the
Grelleberg in Petzow,
dedicated in 1842,
emanates austere majesty.*

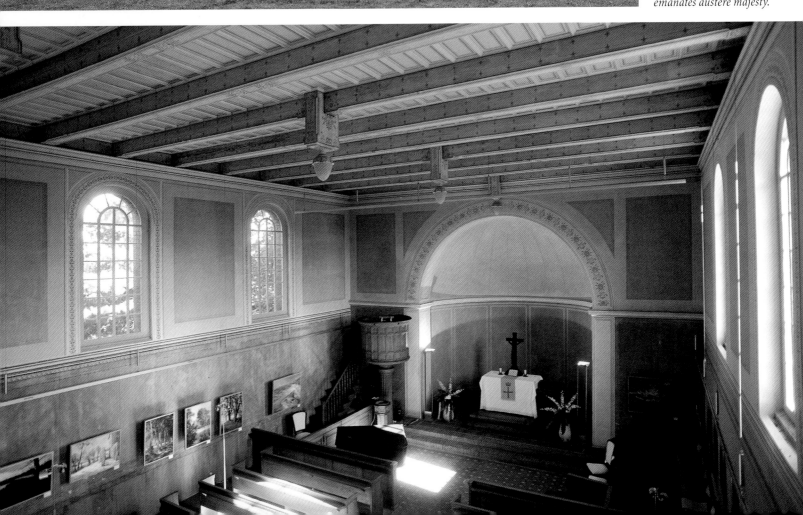

KARL FRIEDRICH SCHINKEL –

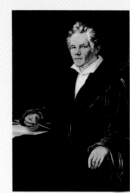

"Man forms himself in all that is beautiful" is one of the maxims of Karl Friedrich Schinkel. Without a foundation in beauty, life is "a mere battle with barbarism." All of the master's works follow this motto.

He was one of the most successful architects of his day: Karl Friedrich Schinkel made a lasting impression on Neo-Classicism in Prussia as an architect, urban planner, painter and designer. He was born on 13 March 1781 in Neuruppin, the town later known as the "city of Fontane." Schinkel's father came from a dynasty of Lutheran pastors. When Karl Friedrich was six years old, on 26 August 1787, a great fire destroyed about two-thirds of the town. The Schinkel family lost all it had; his father died two months later from the strain. In ensuing years, life in Neuruppin was centred on reconstruction.

In 1794, the family moved to Berlin, where Schinkel attended secondary school. Soon, the young man's artistic talent was revealed. He visited many exhibitions; he was deeply impressed by the designs of Friedrich Gilly, who was considered an architectural "Wunderkind." Schinkel wanted to become an architect and became the student and friend of Gilly and his father David Gilly, one of the cofounders of the Berlin Academy of Architecture in 1798. Friedrich Gilly passed away in 1800.

In the years 1803 to 1805, Schinkel travelled in Italy and France; he made countless drawings and sketches of buildings and landscapes. Since the Napoleonic Wars had impoverished Prussia, there were at first few commissions for the young architect, and

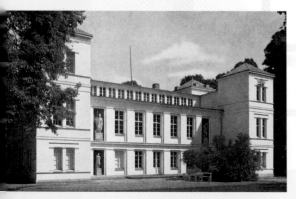

Schinkel earned his living with panoramas and stage sets, of which the "hall of stars" for Mozart's "Magic Flute" (1815) is the most famous yet today.

DESIGN OF THE CAPITAL CITY OF BERLIN

In 1810, he was made a civil servant; finally, in 1838 he gained the rank of director of the Prussian office of public works. As civil servant, he was finally able to dedicate his efforts entirely to architecture. He was not only responsible for designing Berlin as the representative capital city of Prussia, but also for public construction projects in the Prussian territories ranging from the Rhineland to eastern Prussia (today part of Poland and Russia). Every blueprint was submitted to Schinkel, who often made changes. Palaces, churches and monuments were given his touch. In Berlin, he built the Neue Wache in 1816, the Schauspielhaus in 1818, the Alte Museum in 1822, as well as many other public and private buildings. Among those he designed for the members of the Prussian royal family are the palaces Glienicke, Charlottenhof by Sanssouci, Babelsberg and Stolzenfels. Outside Prussia, Schinkel made a name for himself, for instance, with the Elisen Fountain in Aachen and the Hauptwache in Dresden.

We encounter traces of Schinkel everywhere in the march: in Lübbenau and Teltow, Petzow and Gransee, Dennewitz and Seelow, in Cottbus, Liebenwalde and Müncheberg. His chief works include the Neo-Classicist reconstruction of Neuhardenberg Palace – his idea to paint the ceiling of the palace chapel with 6,260 different-sized stars is delightful. Today, clever fundraisers ask visitors to "adopt-a-star" and every euro donated is spent to preserve the building. As early as 1802-03, 21-year-old Schinkel erected his first major work near Neuhardenberg, a caretaker and dairy house in Neo-Romanesque style.

The genius of this man, who died on 13 October 1841, is borne witness by 83 of his own structures, plus dozens of buildings he assisted in planning, 4,000 drawings, 60 oil paintings and 42 stage sets. In addition, he designed interiors and gardens, designed church inventories from the altar to the lamps and practical objects made of the fashionable fine ironwork of the day from garden furniture to tableware to letter openers.

Below left:
In 1765, the von Humboldt family purchased Tegel castle. In the early 19th century, Schinkel was commissioned with the building's renovation and modernization; he transformed it into a Roman-style villa.

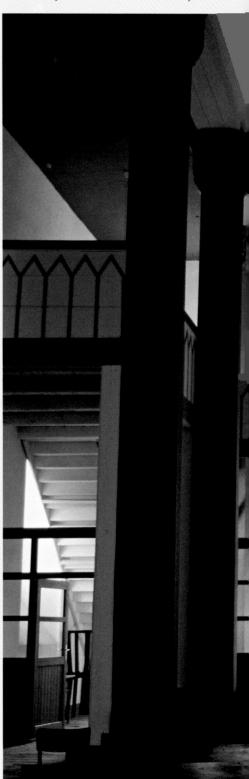

Below:
After a fire in 1817, Schinkel rebuilt the originally Baroque Kreuzkirche in Joachimsthal in the Neo-Gothic style.

Above right:
Straupitz has the march's most important Neo-Classical village church: Schinkel's 1832 design is like a fortress of faith with its two square towers.

Right below:
The village church in Letschin – built in 1818-1819 – was destroyed during the Second World War; only the brick steeple survived.

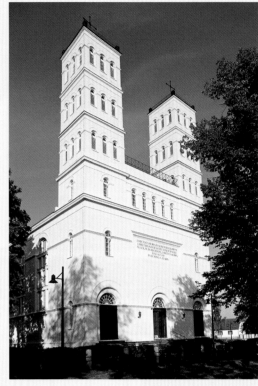

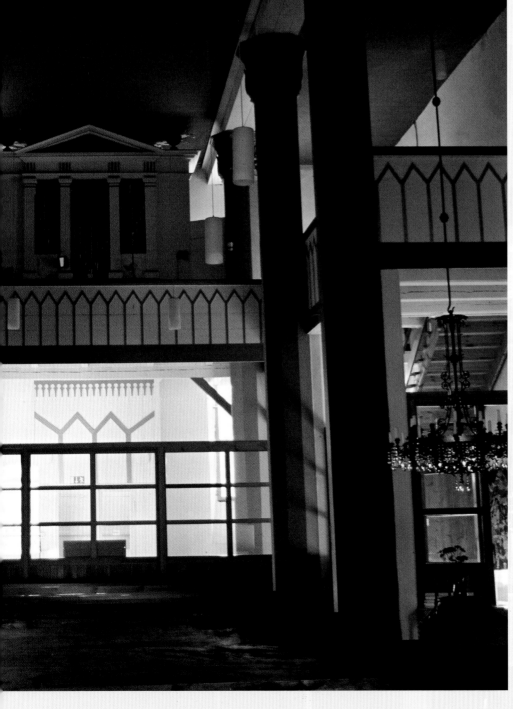

His skills were admired all the way to Vienna and Saint Petersburg, but in particular in Berlin and Brandenburg, his homeland. Theodor Fontane praised him in these words: "Among all the important men brought forth by Ruppin, the town or the county, Karl Friedrich Schinkel is the most important. (…) If Schinkel had never been born, it would have robbed our nonetheless peculiar artistic development of its most crucial moment."

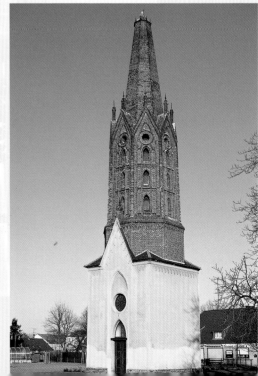

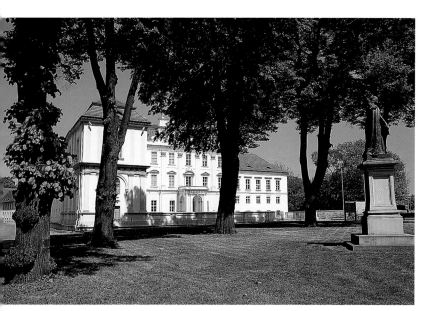

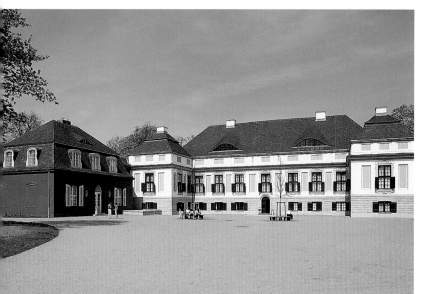

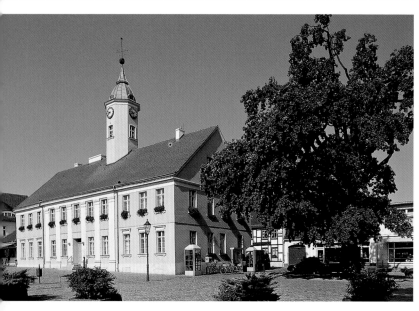

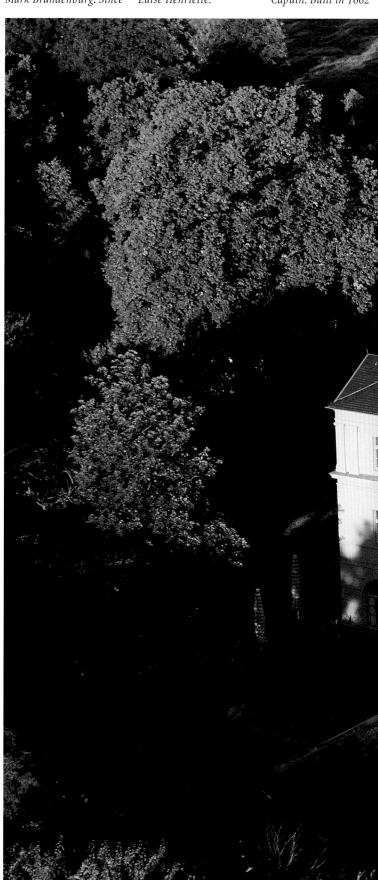

Above left:
"The shape of Oranien-burg Palace in its heyday was that of a Latin H," tells Theodor Fontane in his *Rambles through the Mark Brandenburg*. Since then, it has been rebuilt in its original form and a monument has been set up to the former mistress of the palace, Electress Luise Henriette.

Centre left:
The one-time summer residence of the Great Elector Frederick Willia is on Lake Schwielow in Caputh. Built in 1662

and since then renovated
[i]n an exemplary way),
[t]estifies to the march
[b]aroque. The tiny town
[of] Caputh accommodated
[m]any a great personage:

crowned heads as well as
Charlie Chaplin, Thomas
Mann and Albert Ein-
stein, who owned a sum-
mer cottage in Caputh.

Below left:
Zehdenick once thrived on
industry, but the water-
driven steam hammer,
the brewery and the brick
manufacture are long
still. Today, the friendly
town beckons tourists.

Below:
Ziethen Castle, a former
march manor house from
the 14th century, today
presents itself as a
modern country hotel.
The imposing building is

surrounded by a spacious
park with old stands
of trees. Vacationers
and conference guests
discover a relaxed
atmosphere here.

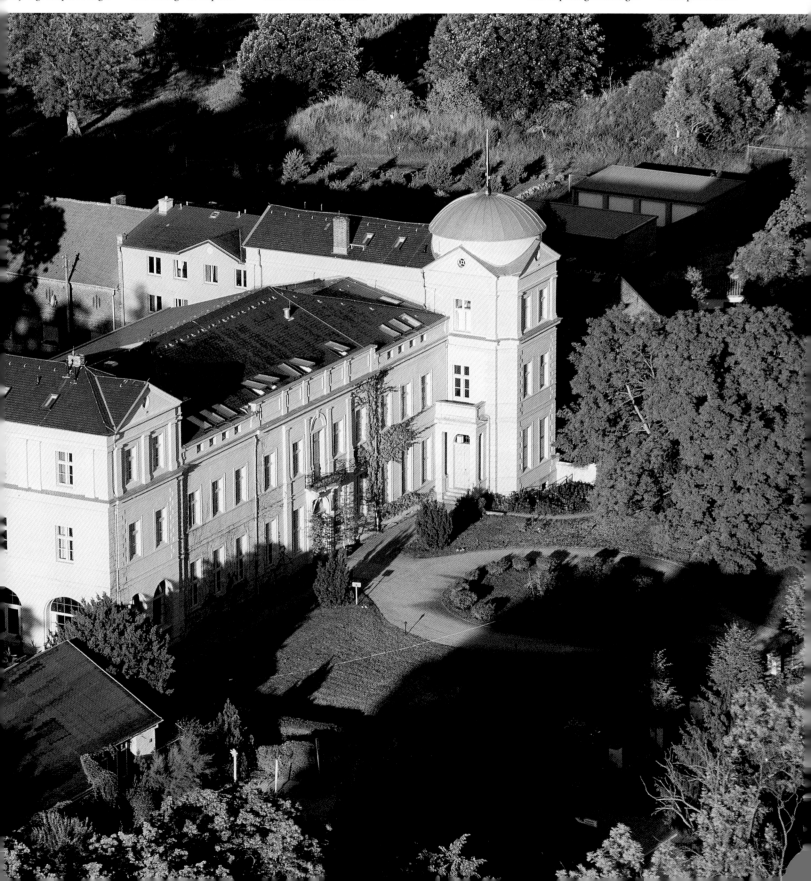

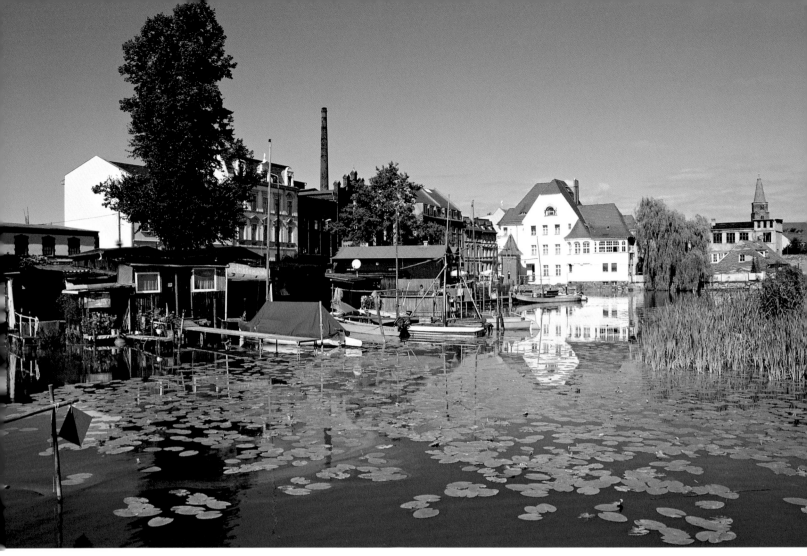

Above and right:
No other German state has as many waters as Brandenburg. What a stimulating adventure to discover the march near Brandenburg on the Havel (above) or near Petzow (right) from the water, whether by ship, yacht, punt or paddleboat.

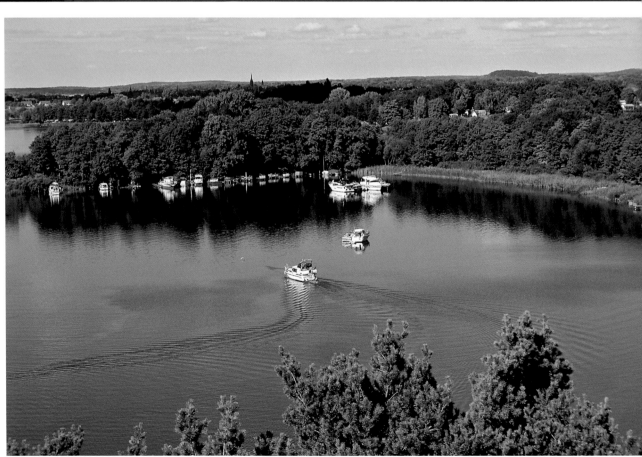

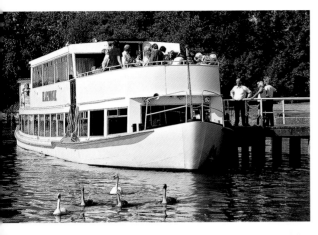

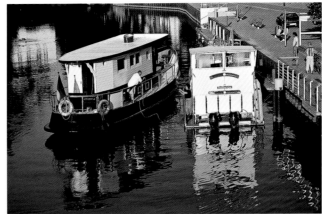

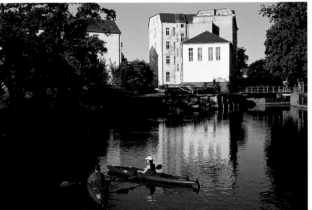

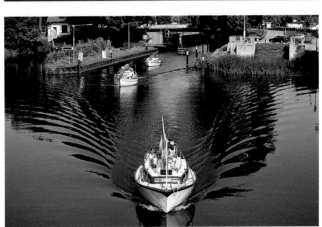

"The Havel," Fontane once remarked, "is a distinctive river... The blue of its water and its many bays (it is actually a chain of lakes) make it unique. The bit of earth that surrounds it, our own Havelland, is ... the site of the most ancient culture in these lands. Here, right on the shores of the river arose the old bishoprics of Brandenburg and Havelberg. And, as the oldest culture was born here, the newest was as well. From Potsdam, Prussia was established, lit by Sanssouci. The Havel can take its place in the ranks of German rivers of culture." – Impressions of Rathenow, Ketzin, Zehdenick and Strodehne.

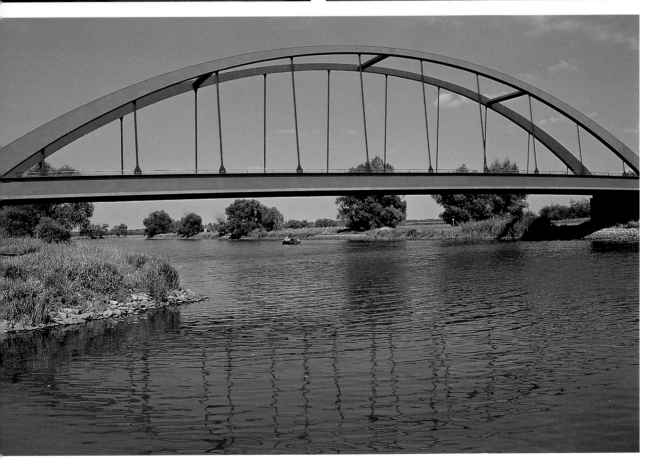

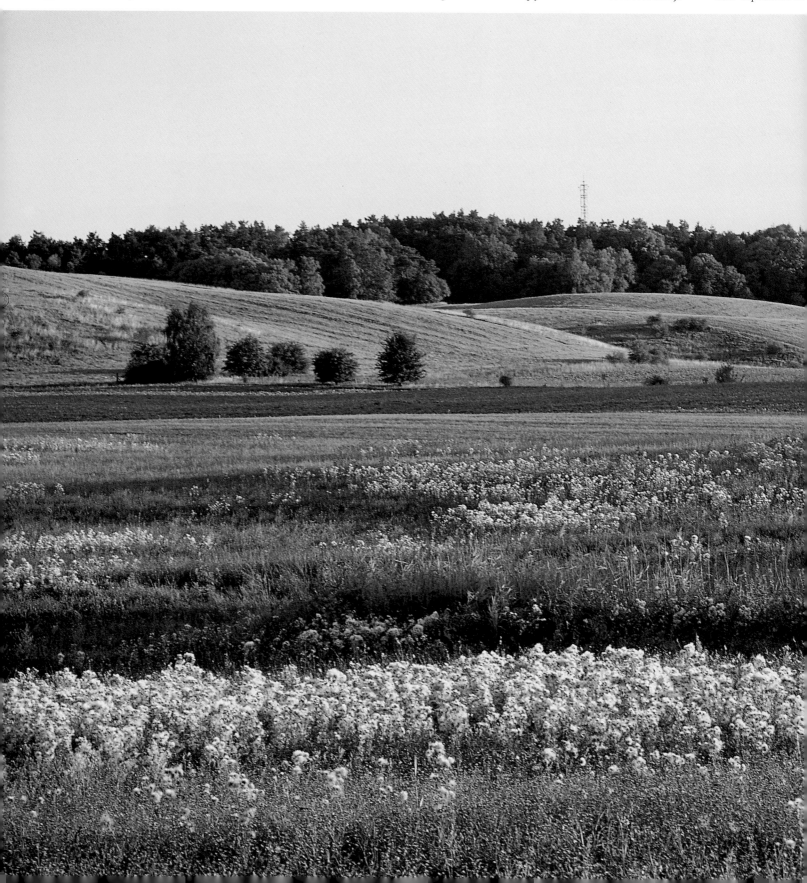

Below:
"Was it beautiful, this landscape? – No: there stood groups of trees, distinguished by nothing, the land began to roll in the distance, hiding a coppice and revealing another – we were glad that it had basically everything …"A harsh song of praise by Kurt Tucholsky to the sometimes harsh landscape of Brandenburg, here by Klein Ziethen.

Above right:
A site of horror: In 1936, the National Socialists opened Sachsenhausen concentration camp. A memorial commemorates the hundreds of thousands who met their horrific deaths here – and reminds us that after the war, the Soviet occupiers used the camp for their own purposes as well. About ten thousand opponents of the Communists were murdered here in absurd continuity.

Centre right:
Perhaps in his solitary rambles Albert Einstein walked along this pathway on Lake Templin near Caputh. He on

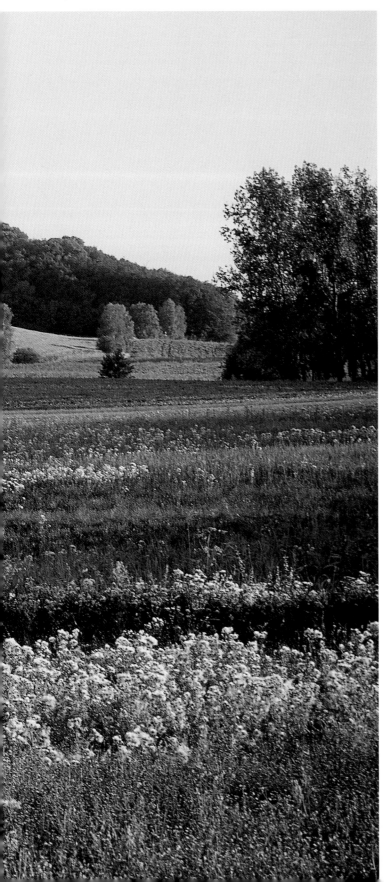

Below right:
From Easter 1894, Otto Lilienthal, the modern Icarus, used the Gollenberg near Stölln regularly for his flight attempts. On 9 August 1896, a sun squall (an abrupt shift of warm air from the ground) threw him a loop above the Rhinow hills. He plummeted and died the next day. He is remembered not only by this monument; a museum as well records his life.

said of Caputh: "The sailing ship, the view, the solitary autumn walks, the relative quiet; it is a paradise."

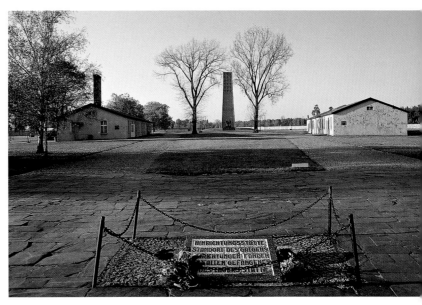

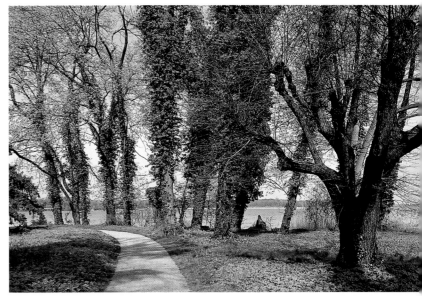

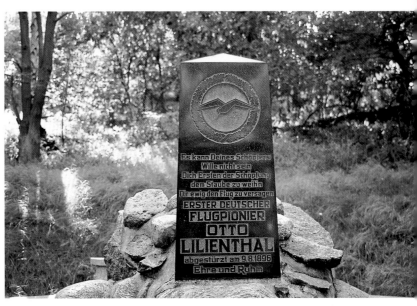

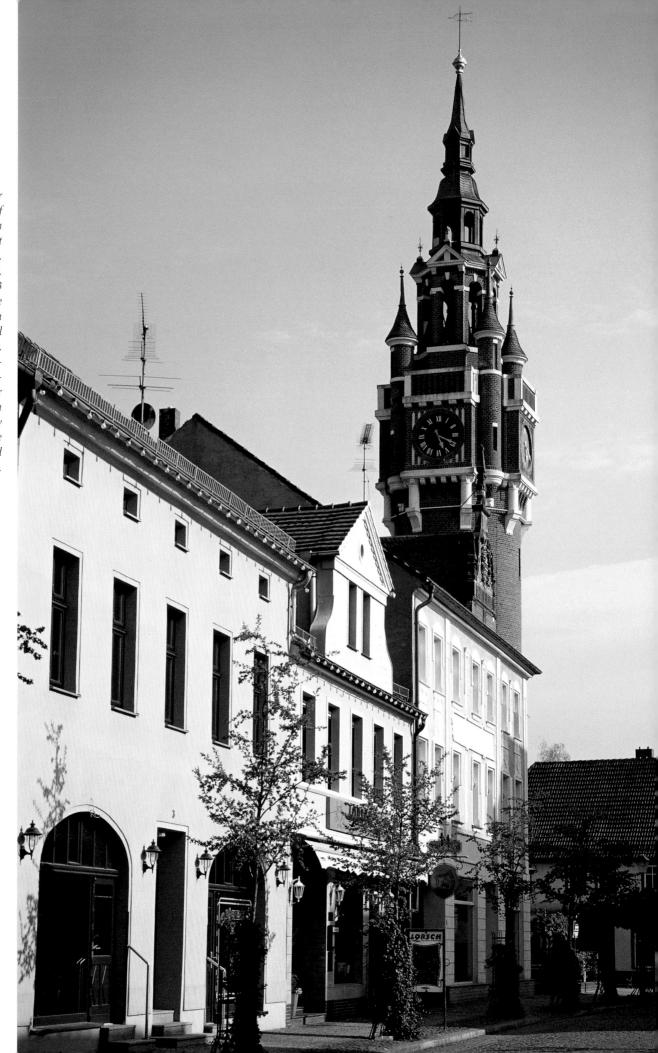

In its almost 850-year history, the town of Dahme burned down seven times. Today, it stands chic and shining. Its gem is the town hall. It was erected from 1893 to 1894 on the site of the old Nikolaikirche, which was used as town hall after the Reformation. The 47 meter (155 foot)-high tower was imaginatively designed. Whoever mounts its 119 steps can enjoy a panorama view of the little town and the surrounding fields and forests.

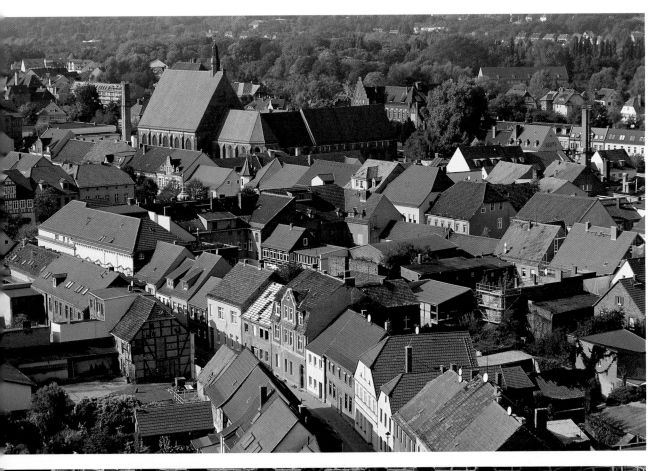

Jüterbog displays an impressive medieval ensemble. According to legend, the town is said to have its name from its first visitor, who once strode through one of the three formidable city gates. It was a little old lady, "Jutte with the Billy goat." Once a splendid town of trades and crafts, in Prussian days Jüterbog was a garrison town.

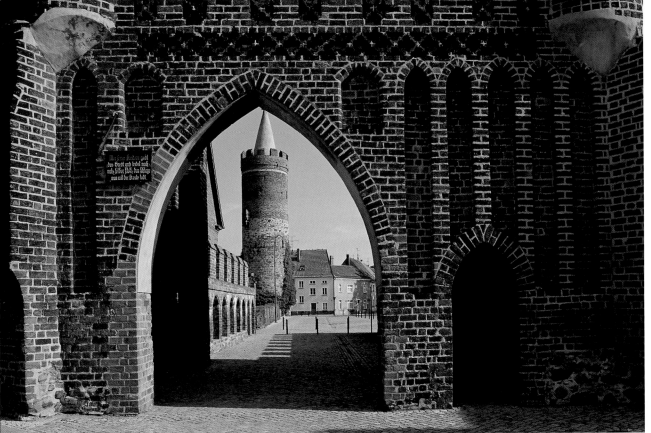

Then as today: whoever passes through the Damm Gate dating from 1300 is received by lovely Jüterbog with all sorts of sights and busy small town life.

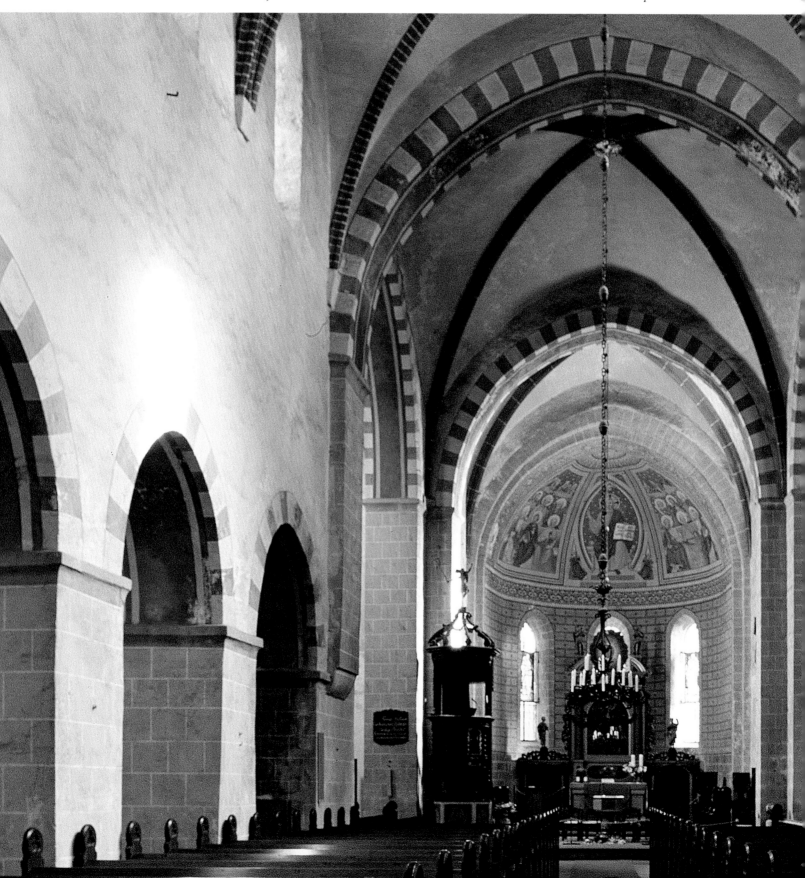

Below:
In 1170, the Rhenish Altenberg Monastery established a monastery at Zinna. The monastery church built of hewn boulders has a turbulent history behind it but today is again a place of meditation.

Above right:
The Reformation sealed the fate of Zinna Monastery. The Cistercian abbey was dissolved in 1553. A weavers' settlement was set up near the former abbey; th monastery buildings wer used as a quarry. Late the Royal Regional Cour was housed here an from 1956 a local histor museum.

Centre right:
The main street in Treuenbrietzen is as oad as the Ku'damm in rlin! The history of the town's name, its sights and the gruesome ballad of "Sabinchen" can be found at the local history museum in the former Holy Ghost Chapel, a tower in the town walls.

Below right:
Practical collaboration: the massive, freestanding market tower in Luckenwalde has been used by the nearby Church of St. John as bell tower since 1484.

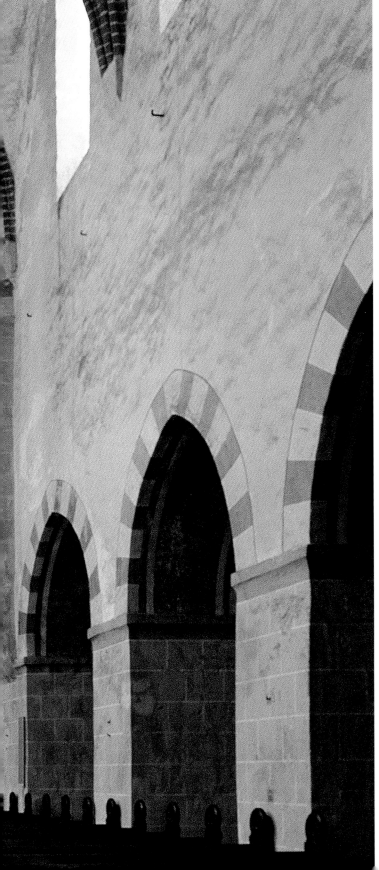

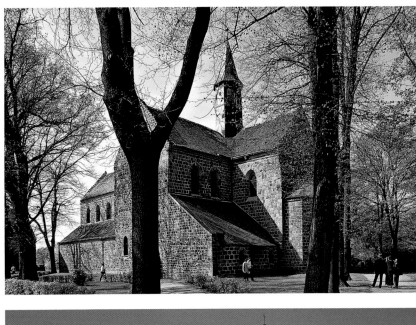

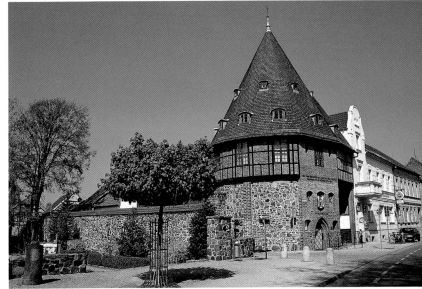

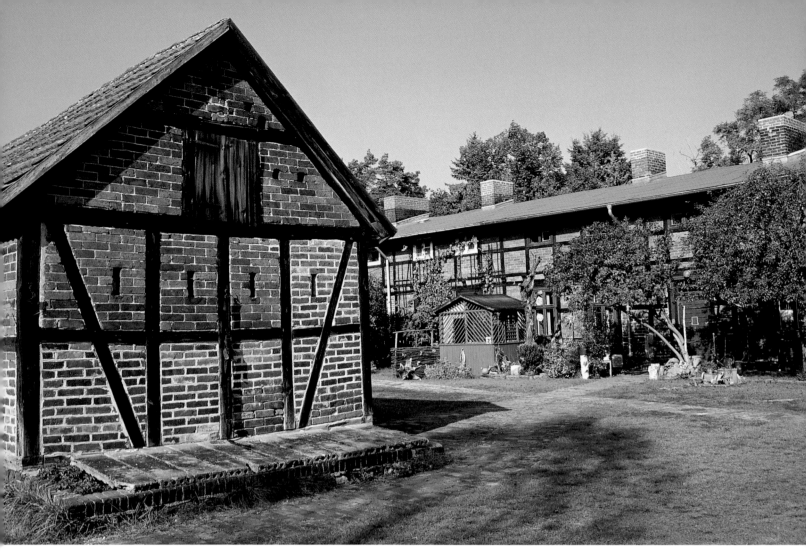

Above and right:
The glassblower Reinhold Burger from Baruth in Brandenburg gave the world a valuable invention – the thermos bottle! At Museumsdorf Baruther Glashütte, we find interesting facts of his life and the history of glass production there, once famed for its lampshades and cylinders and fermenting bottles. Even today, we can watch glassblowers at work here or learn something about the process of sausage smoking.

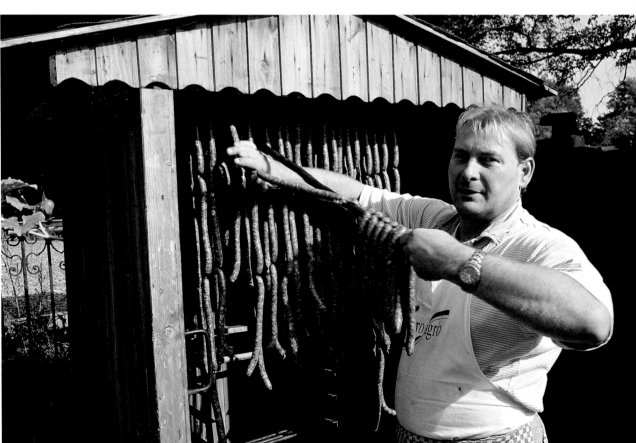

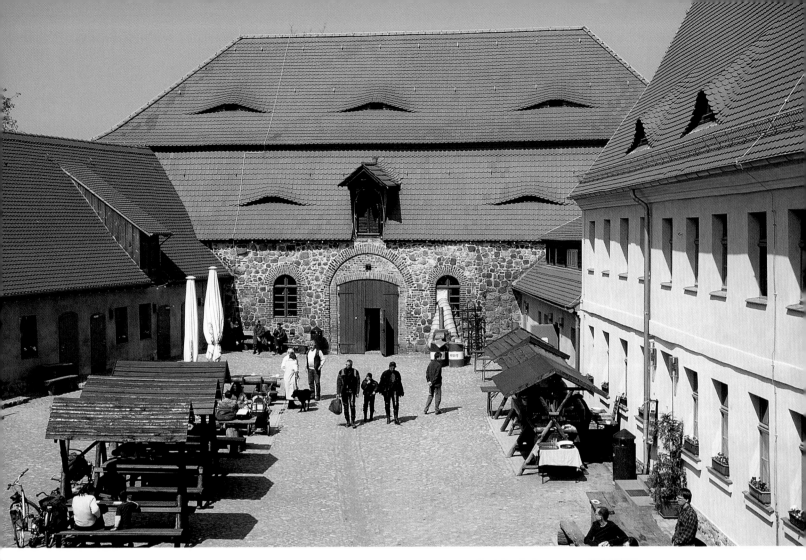

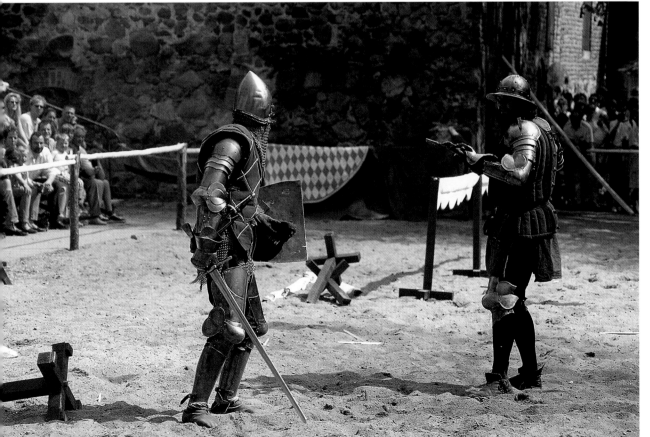

Above:
Above the village of Raben rises proud Rabenstein Castle, which was built in the mid-12th century to guard the streets. Its location and sturdy defensive structures long made Rabenstein impenetrable. Its cellars could hold large amounts of stores; the only thing the castle lacked was a well. The castle has been used as a youth hostel since 1956.

Left:
Rabenstein Castle is the site of many annual medieval festivals, such as those at Advent, Easter and Whitsun; the castle is also a popular movie backdrop.

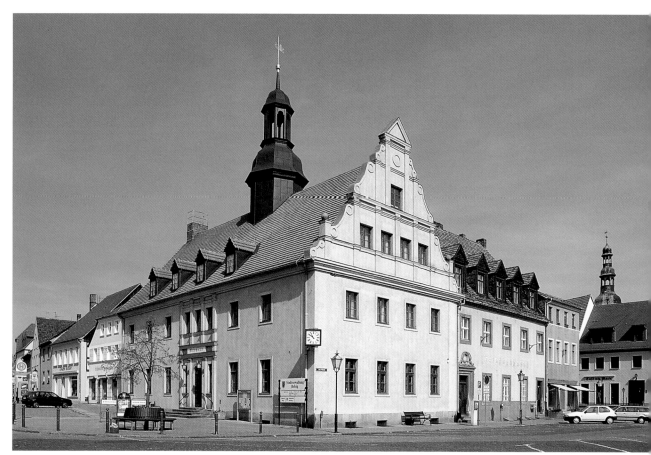

Right:
The town hall at Belzig, a two-storey rendered building with decorative gable, was once a Saxon office. However, in the battle on the Hagelberg in 1813, the town came under Prussian rule. Belzig became an accredited resort in 2002. The former lung sanatorium from 1900 is now a modern rehabilitation clinic called "Hoher Fläming."

Below:
Eisenhardt Castle in Belzig is more than one thousand years old. In the 15th century, it was expanded to a fortress with the addition of a circular wall and round towers. Today, the building houses a hotel and a local history museum.

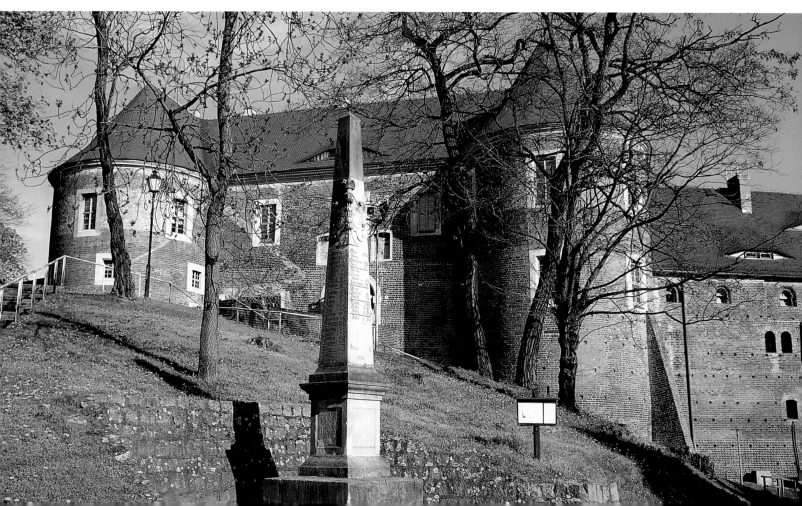

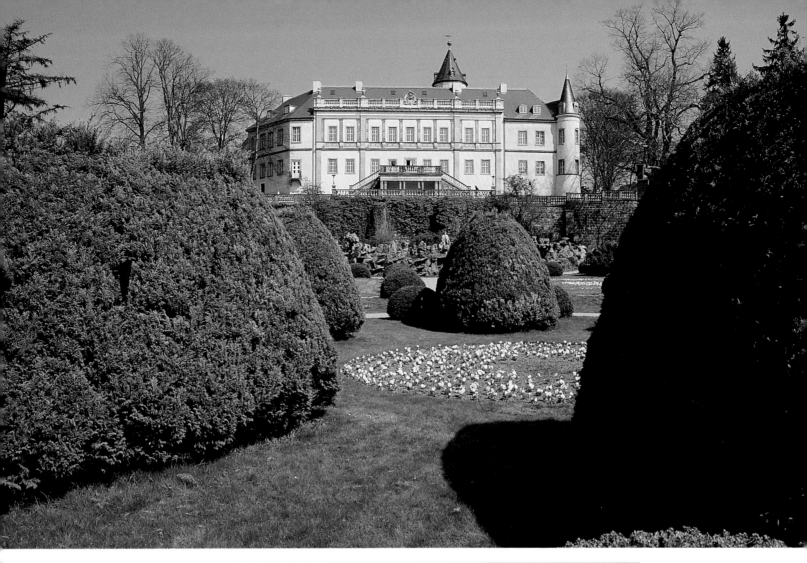

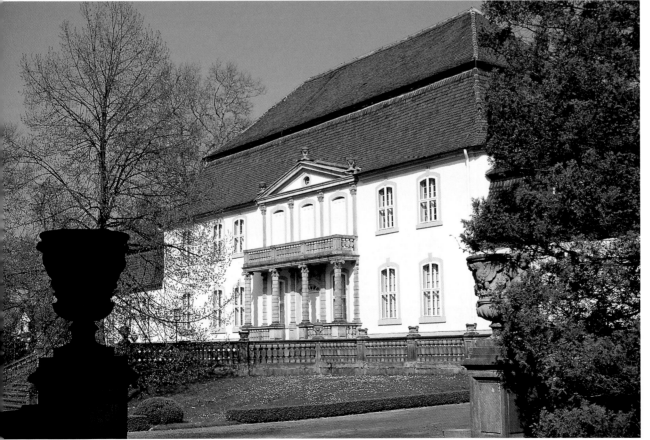

Above:
Like so often in Brandenburg: far from the towns, we are surprised by imposing palaces and gardens. Wiesenburg originated in the 12th century, was modernized in the Renaissance style and perfectly restored since reunification.

Left:
In the 19th century, Wiepersdorf Palace was the home of the poet couple Bettina and Achim von Arnim. The regal house with the imposing grounds, the peaceful country life – must that not have been the source of inspiration? Bettina once complained: "You forget how to write here, where all day, all year, your whole life long nothing happens to make you lift an arm or a leg."

61

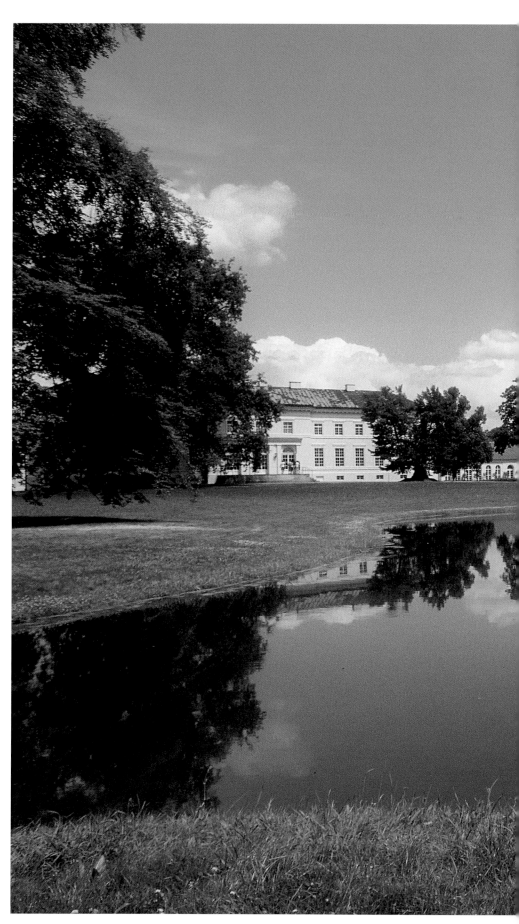

Brandenburg's southeast holds no natural spectacles, making it typical for the march. The Spreewald, the lakes Schwieloch and Scharmützel (the "March Sea"), Schlaube Valley and the Märkische Schweiz around Buckow – it is the water that makes these areas a holiday paradise.

The cities of Cottbus and Frankfurt an der Oder are the regional centres. Reconstruction of the Marienkirche in Frankfurt, destroyed during the war, was a model of grassroots perseverance: the Party aimed to have the monument to what it considered an outdated social order removed, but courageous citizens of Frankfurt fought for its preservation with zeal and cunning. Garden lovers will appreciate Cottbus for Branitzer Park and the park along the shores of the Spree River, which in 1995 was the showplace of the first Federal Garden Show to be held in one of the "new" federal states after reunification.

The town centres of Peitz, Luckau, Beeskow and Bad Freienwalde offer medieval flair. Every summer, Gross-Leuthen gets very modern: during the "Rohkunstbau" campaign, exhibitions by contemporary international artists are organized in the castle of this Spreewald village. Guests from around the world come to the "Eurospeedway" racetrack in Lusatia; however, this most expensive construction project of the state of Brandenburg has not yet reaped the anticipated economic success. By contrast, the "Tropical Islands" by Staakow are a complete success. In a former zeppelin hangar – the world's largest self-supporting hall –, resourceful entrepreneurs created a fun pool that offers something for everyone with an artificial beach, lagoons, rain forest and exotic shows.

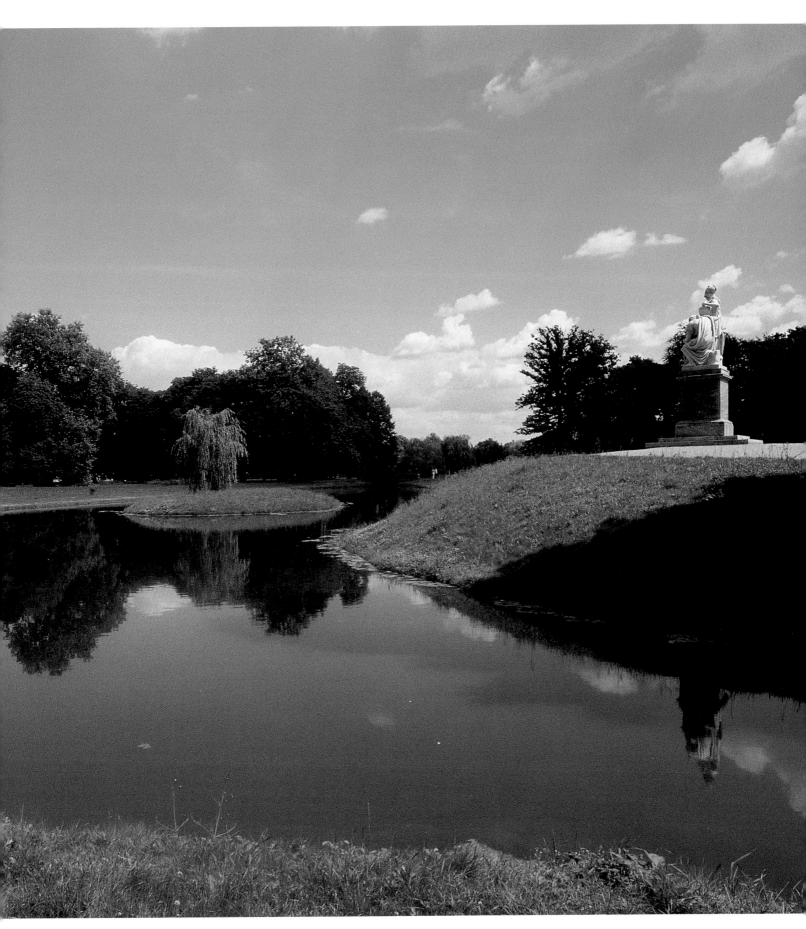

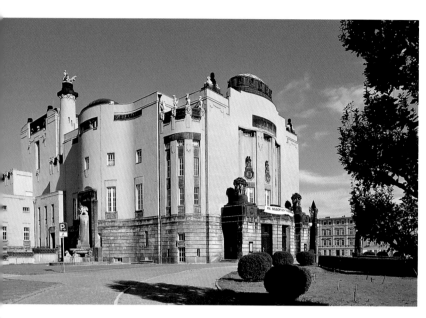

Above left:
Cottbus may be situated in the province, but its state theatre on Schiller-platz is metropolitan: the handsome Jugendstil building, constructed in 1907-1908 by the Berlin architect Bernhard Sehring, is the venue for operas, plays and ballets of highest quality.

Centre left:
In 1995, the Federal Garden Show attracted many visitors from western Germany to Cottbu. They were able to discover not only magnifi

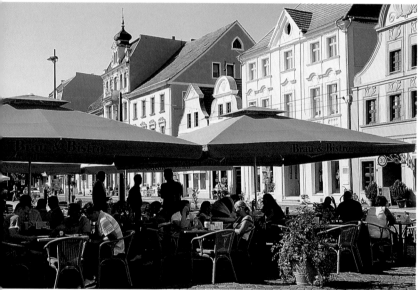

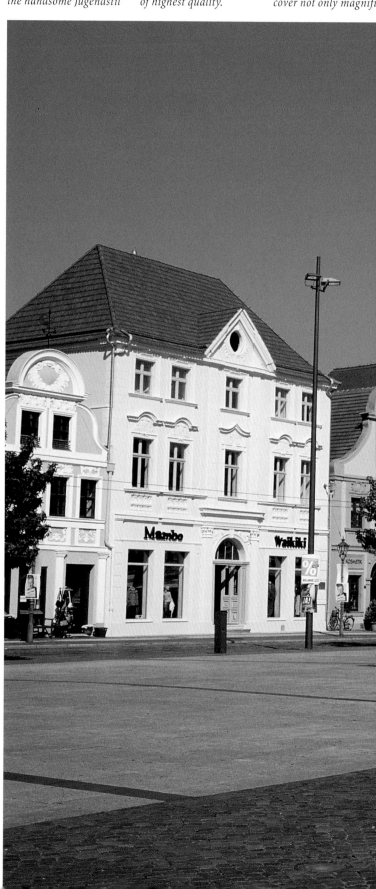

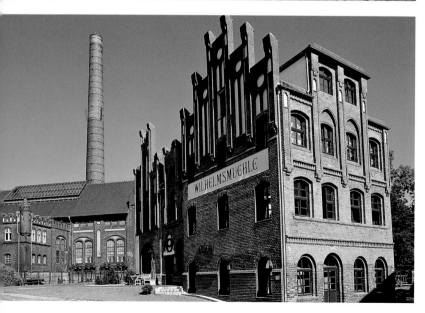

...nt parks, but also a city ...th a long history. In ...e Middle Ages, cloth ...s produced here, later ...e Huguenots intro-...ced silk weaving and

after the war, Cottbus developed into the region's centre of lignite mining. Today, the city is the seat of Brandenburg Technical University.

Below left:
Cottbus has many sights to offer, like a Sorb Museum and a collection of contemporary art, plus churches and towers.

Today, the historic power plant of 1903 with its Neo-Gothic battlements is a venue for all types of cultural events.

Below:
The Altmarkt (old mar-ketplace) is the "front parlour" of Cottbus, the centre of Lower Lusatia, called Chosebuz in

Sorbian. Brandenburg's second-largest city was once an important stopover on the Salt Route from Halle to Silesia.

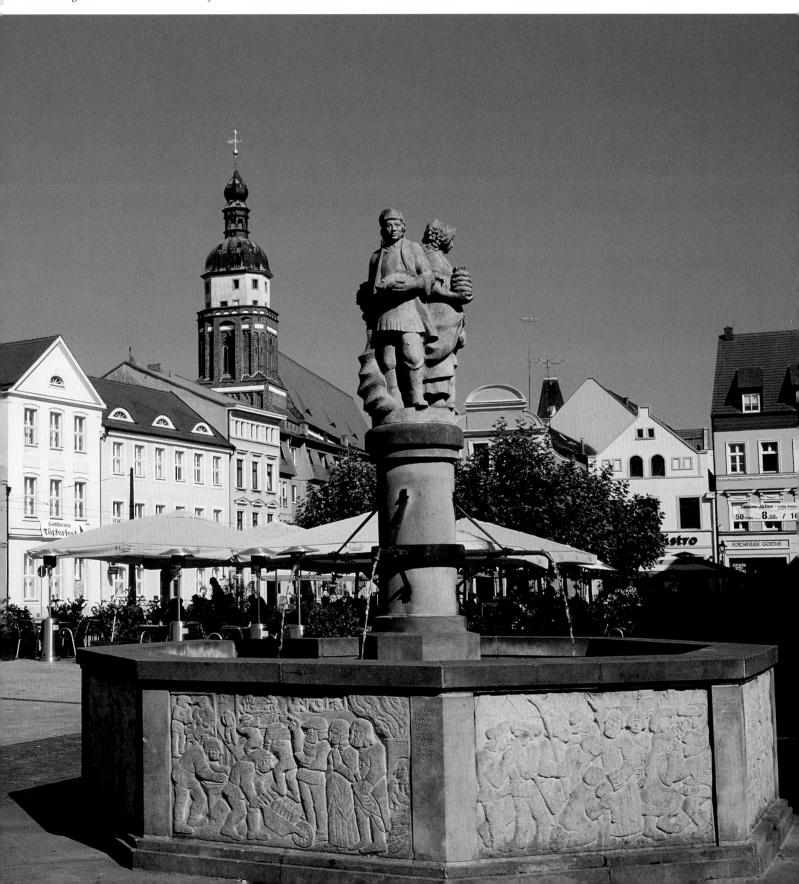

Below:
In Babelsberg, Muskau and Branitz, Prince Pückler had splendid parks laid out. The gifted landscape architect spared no pains to have the sandy march soil removed and to create artificial lakes. In Branitz, he even erected two pyramids, the stepped Land Pyramid and the Water Pyramid in which the prince and his wife were laid to rest.

Right:
Prince Hermann von Pückler-Muskau was a playboy, adventurer, garden enthusiast and author. His travelogues made him famous; his novels (some published anonymously or under a pseudonym) caused uproars. An exhibition in Branitz Palace near Cottbus reports about his remarkable life.

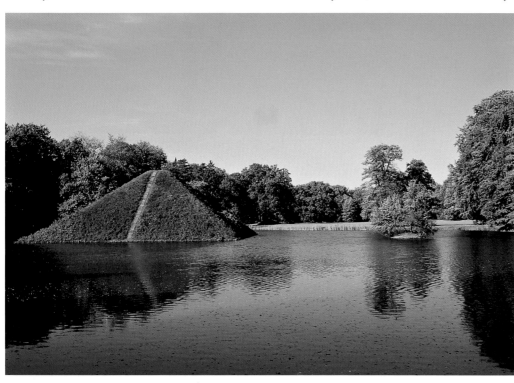

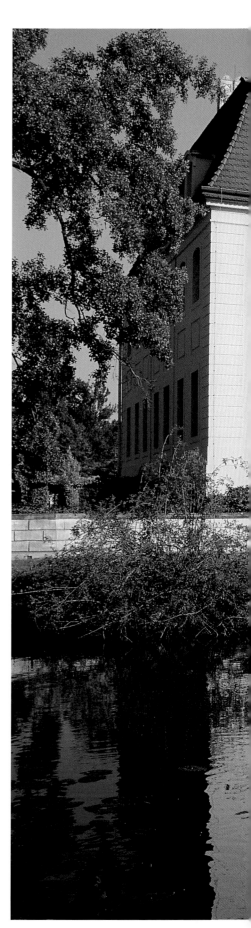

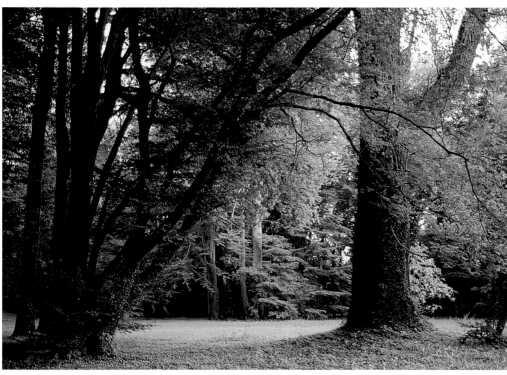

Above:
The idyllic gardens of Branitz are a unique work of art from the hand of Hermann von Pückler-Muskau (1785–1871) and his successor Count Heinrich von Pückler (1835–1897).

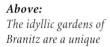

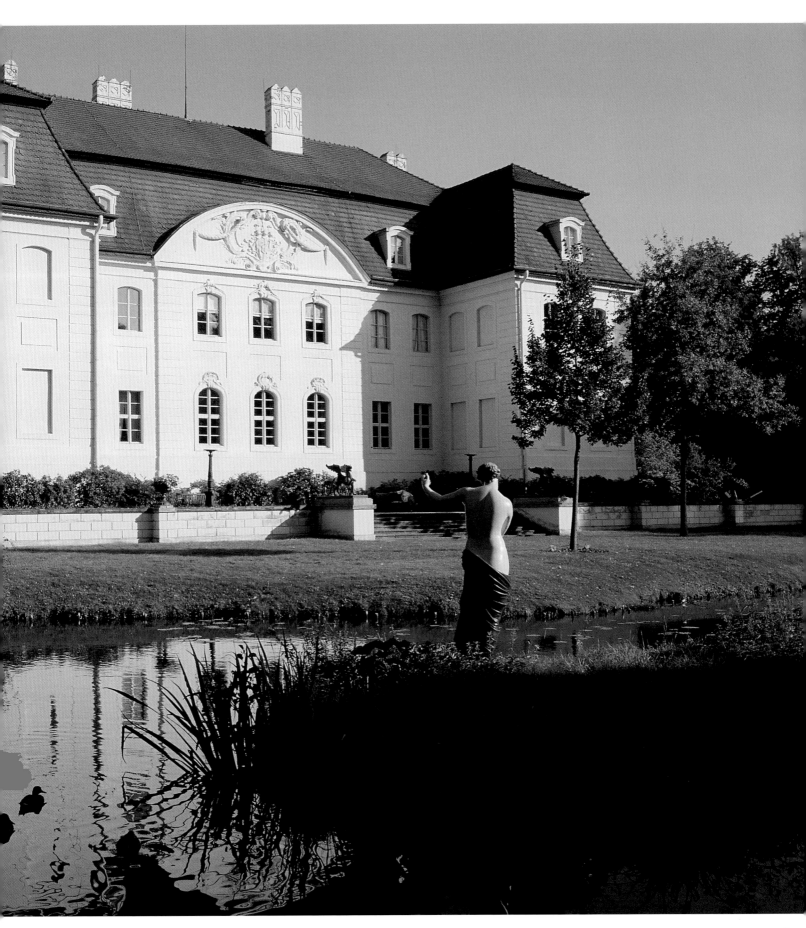

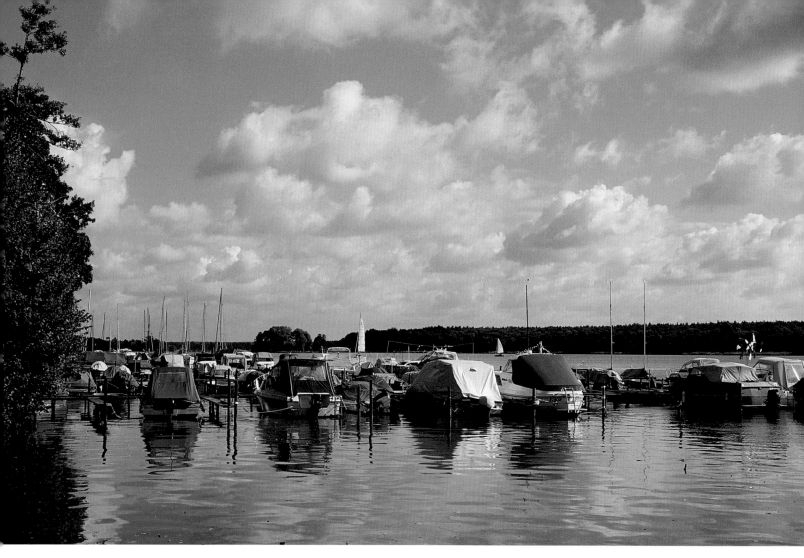

Above:
How idyllic: clouds passing unhurriedly over Lake Zeuthen.

Right:
The manor houses found all over the state of Brandenburg – such as Geisenhof in Lower Lusatia – testify to the economic prosperity that once prevailed here. During the Socialist phase many splendid structures fell to ruin, yet are now being restored.

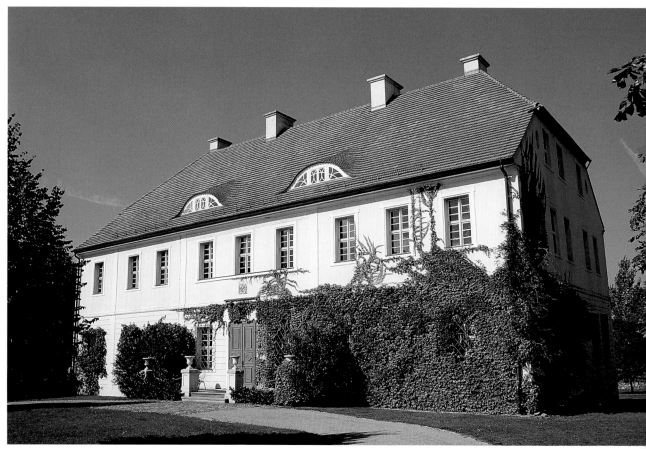

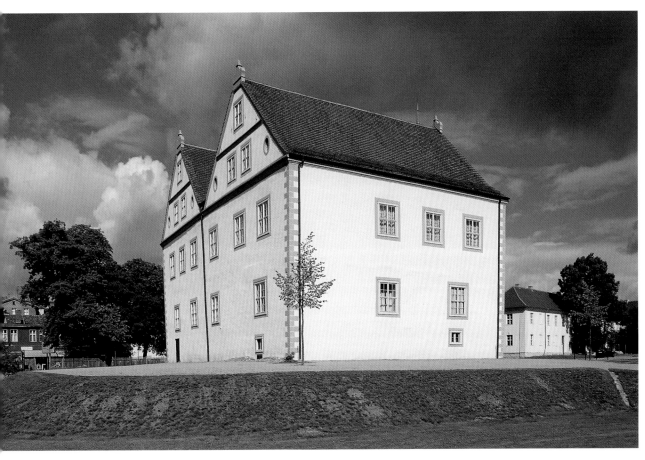

Left:
The castle of Königs Wusterhausen, an autumn residence of the soldier king Frederick I, seems very plain especially from the rear. The father of Old Fritz met here with high-ranking personages for his "tobacco collegium," a moderate round of debates. – Königs Wusterhausen is considered the cradle of German radio: the first broadcast, a Christmas concert, was carried on the airwaves from the radio station on 22 December 1920.

Below:
During the Socialist era, Gottfried Benn complained that the poorest German suit fabric came from Spremberg. Today, "the pearl of Lower Lusatia" is a Brandenburg gem.

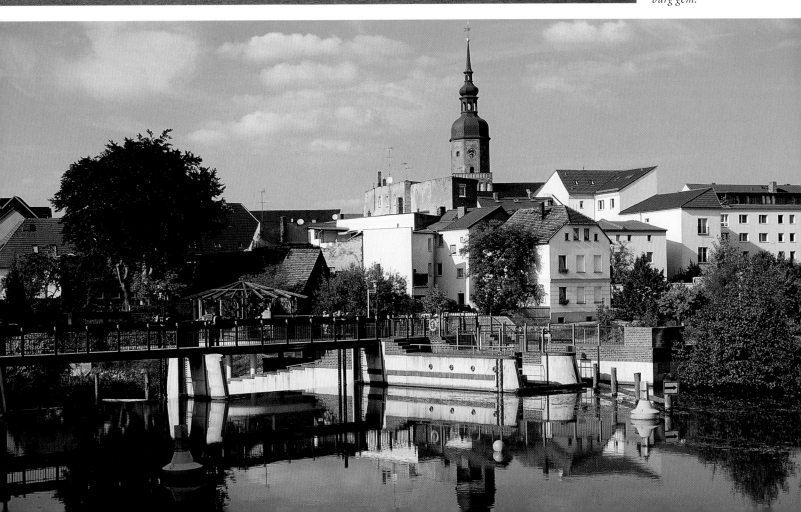

Right:

Fürstlich Drehna, first documented in 1301, is now part of the city of Luckau. Its most important building is the moated castle, which was repeatedly expanded and modified upon the remains of its medieval predecessor until the late 19th century.

Far right:

The Renaissance palace in Doberlug-Kirchhain was given its present appearance in the second half of the 17th century.

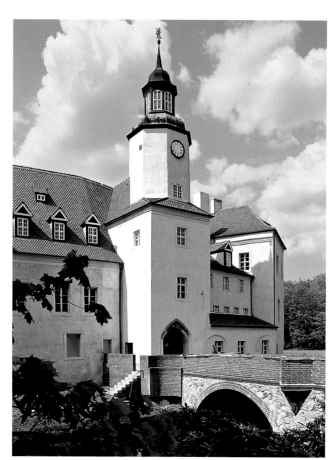

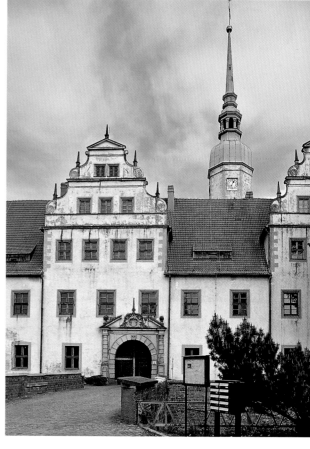

Right:

Luckau's heyday is over; the decorative gabled houses and St. George's Chapel, whose 47 meter (155 foot)-high Hausmannsturm once housed the tower trumpeter, originated during its significant epoch as a trading city.

Far right:

Come in, it is worth it! The former monastery in Doberlug and its church have gone through hard times: in 1431, the structure was destroyed by the Hussites, then by the Swedes in the Thirty Years' War. Additions and modifications have gone on until the present.

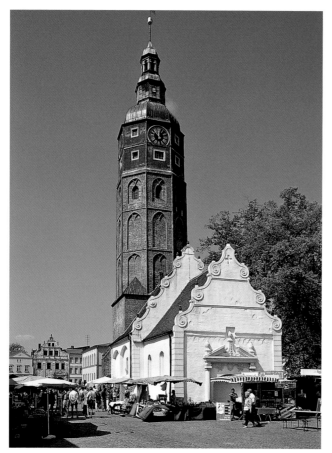

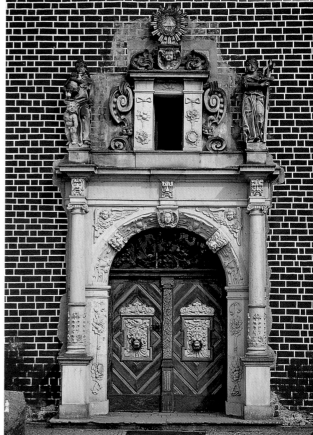

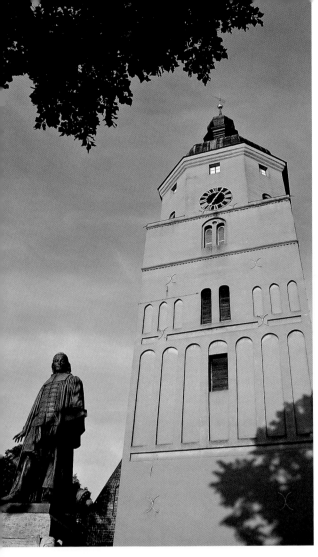

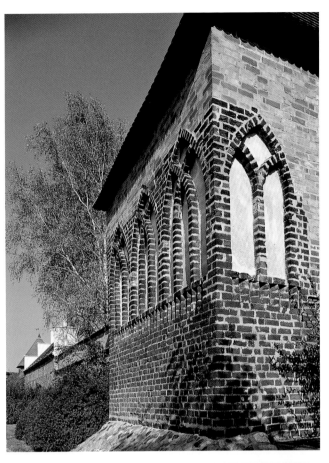

Far left:
This church in Lübben in the Spreewald is named after the "sweet singer of Lutheranism," the writer of such well-known hymns as "Awake, My Heart with Gladness," "O Sacred Head, Now Wounded" and "Commit Thou All Thy Griefs," Paul Gerhardt. With his approximately 135 hymns, Gerhardt is among the best-known poets of Protestant song, after Martin Luther. Lübben was his last home until he died there in 1676.

Left:
Parts of the medieval city wall of Lübben have been preserved.

Left:
Lübben, as well, has a small castle, which today houses a modern town and regional museum.

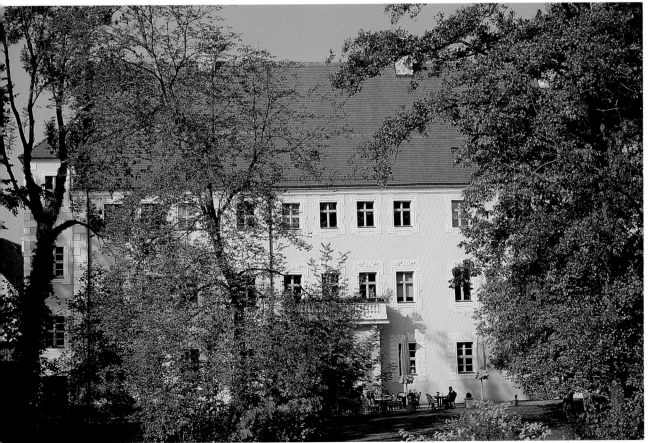

Pages 72/73:
In his Rambles through the Mark Brandenburg Theodor Fontane noted: "We reached Lehde, the first Spreewald village. It is a pocket version of the lagoon city, a Venice, as it may have been 1,500 years ago when the first fishing families sought refuge on its swampy isles. You have seen nothing more charming than this Lehde, made of as many islands as it has houses."

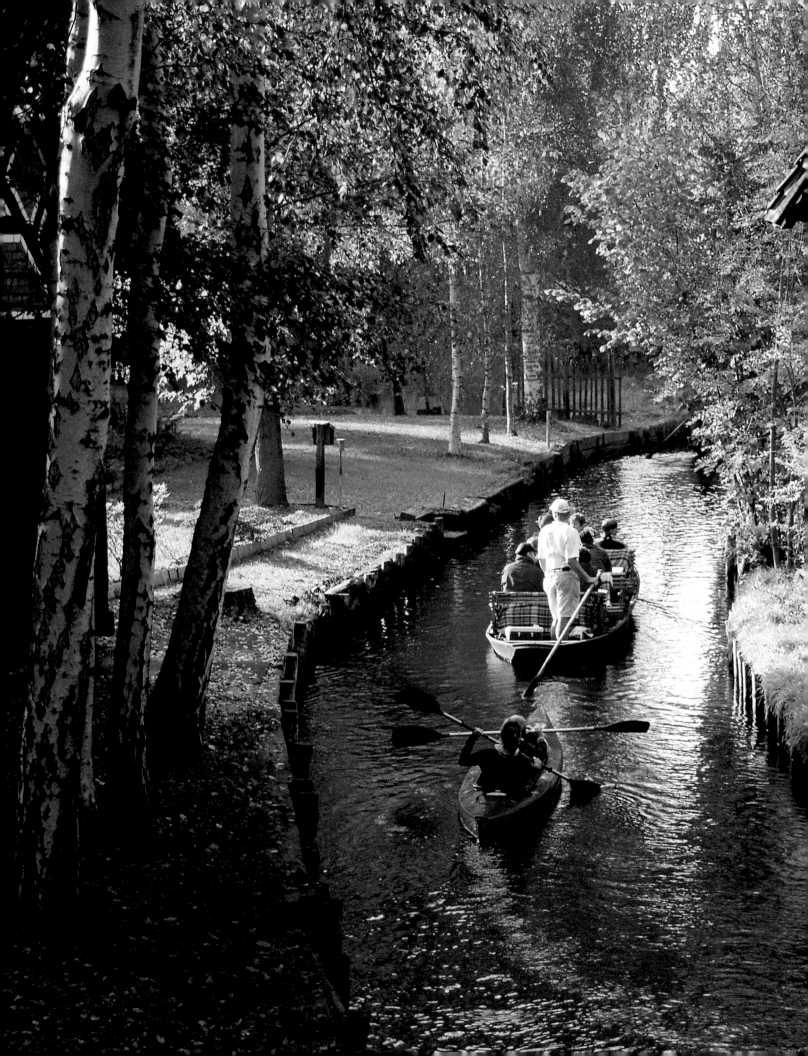

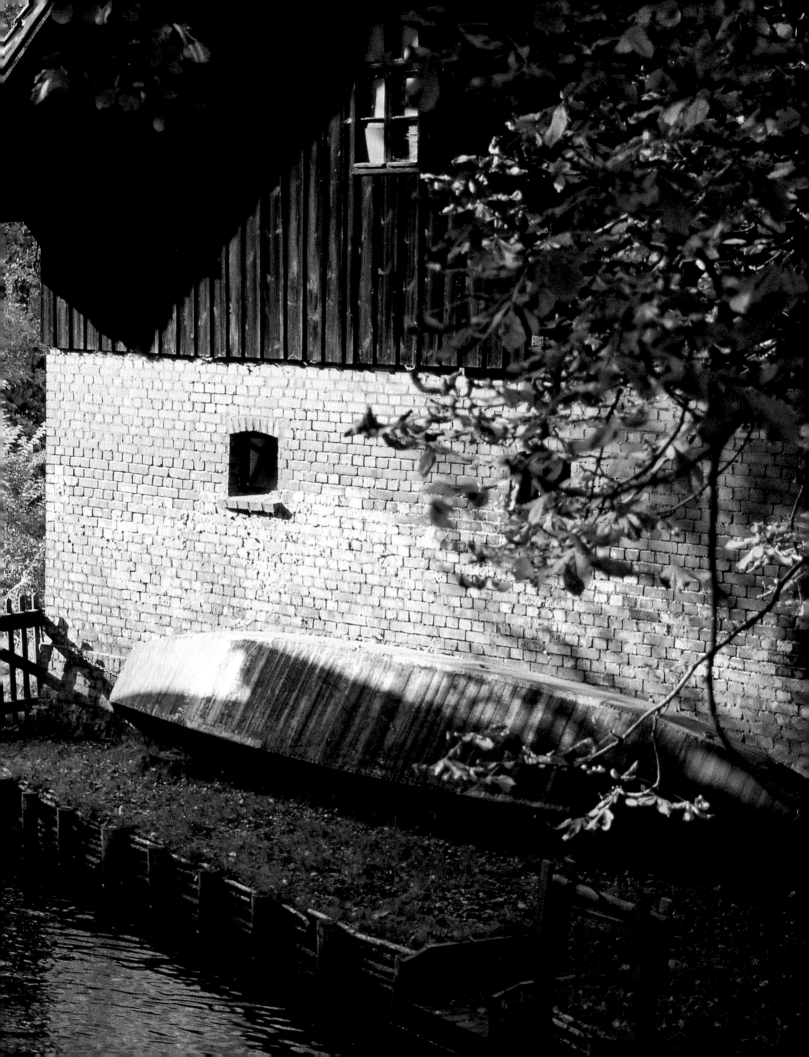

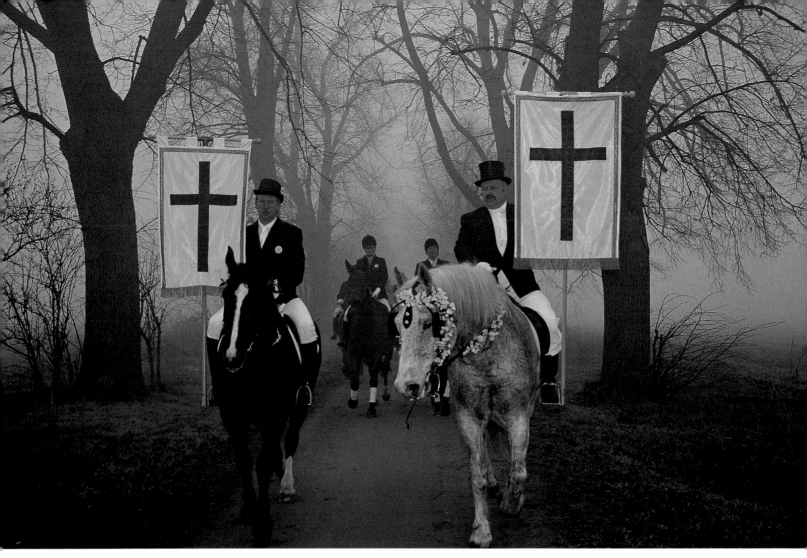

Above:
Every Easter Sunday at ten o'clock, the traditional Easter ride, a ceremonial procession on horseback, takes place in Zerkwitz.

Right and far right:
For experts, the traditional costume is like a passport: they can tell what part of the Spreewald the wearer comes from. Travellers usually can only see the intricate blouses, skirts, aprons and bonnets at the museum in Lehde, yet there are still a few "genuine" costume wearers. Parties and celebrations are reasons to dress up.

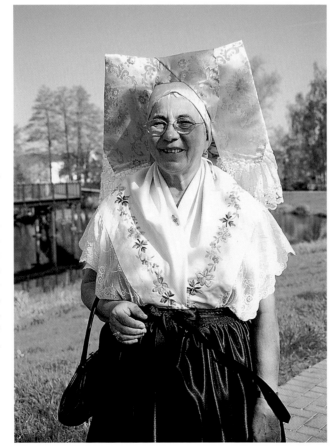

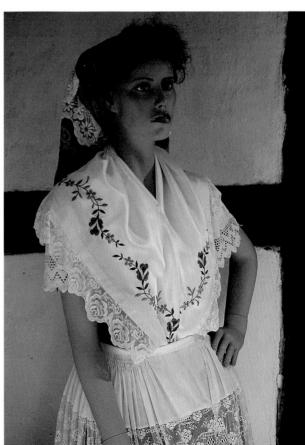

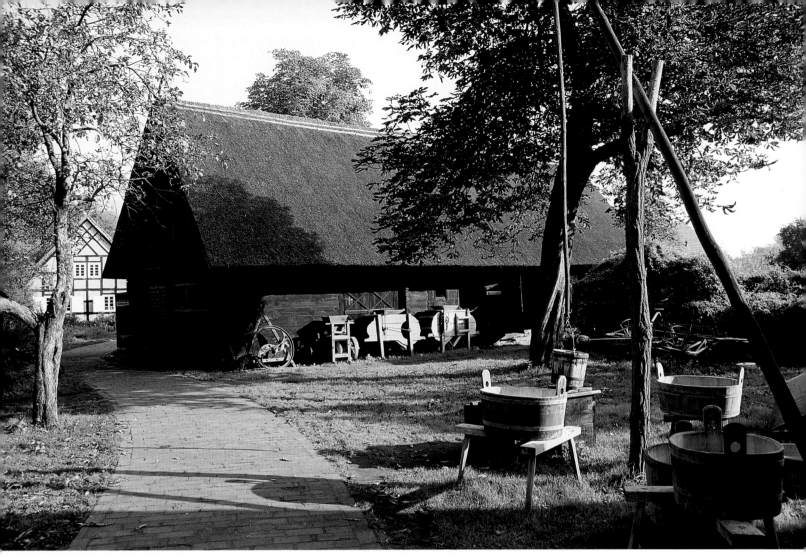

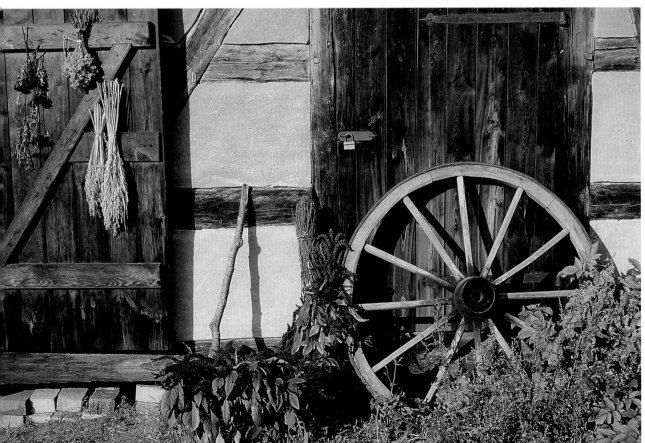

Even after the war, the
Sorbs in the Spreewald
lived under almost
medieval conditions, far
from the loud and hectic
world around them.
The museum in Lehde
illustrates their daily
lives and religious
customs. The present has
long reached even the
Spreewald – with all its
blessings and problems.

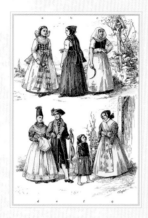

A traditional costume standardizes the form, colour and manner of wearing a society's clothing, leaving little room for individual fashion or style. Instead, it bonds a group of people – like the Sorbs – together.

On a visit to Cottbus, one notices the word "Chośebuz" on all official signs bearing the city's name. This is the name of the town in the language of the native people of Lusatia: the Sorbs. Historically, the Sorbs settled in the area ranging from Upper Lusatia in Saxony – in particular the region between the district capitals of Bautzen, Kamenz and Hoyerswerda – and Lower Lusatia in southern Brandenburg. There, they live around about Cottbus and in the Spreewald, between Senftenberg in the south and Lübben in the north.

The Sorbs are a western Slavic people that never founded their own state. As early as the seventh century, Sorbs migrated to the

larger numbers of Germans. Only in Lusatia were they able to preserve their Sorbian identity.

This identity is based primarily on their language. For the Sorbs, language is the decisive criterion of belonging. The two cultural centres in Bautzen in Upper and Cottbus in Lower Lusatia led to the development of two closely related yet different languages by the 19th century: Upper Sorbian, related to Czech, and Lower Sorbian, related to Polish. The Lower Sorbs also call themselves Wends, while the Upper Sorbs do not use this name. The number of active speakers is estimated at about 30,000. Today, all of these speakers also speak German. In the state of Brandenburg, pupils learn Sorbian at 26 elementary schools and 1 high school; however, lessons are no longer given in the mother tongue. Sorbian newspapers, magazines and books, radio and television programmes keep the language alive.

ZAPUST AND PLUCKING THE COCK

Under Nazi rule, the use of Sorbian in public was banned. In the GDR, the Sorbs were permitted to preserve their national customs and traditions. After German reunification, their rights as a national minority were acknowledged and preservation of

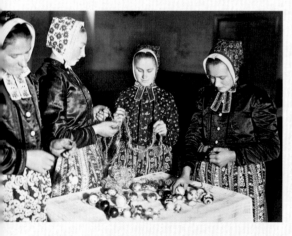

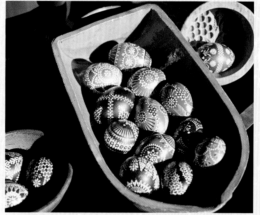

land between the Baltic Sea and Erzgebirge (Ore Mountains). When the region was conquered by King Henry I in the year 929, they came under German rule; after the founding of the Meissen bishopric in 968, they were Christianized. The immigration of German peasants from the west resulted in a blending of the peoples; by the end of the Middle Ages, the Sorbs had been assimilated by the

their traditions experienced another renaissance within families, villages, clubs and churches. Sorb costumes can be admired at festivals and celebrations. The calendar includes customs such as "Zapust" (Lower Sorbian Shrovetide) or "rooster plucking" after the harvest. Sorb choruses, dance troupes and theatres testify to the Sorb culture. Their famous writers include Jurij Brězan.

Far left:
Once, Sorbian women wore white scarves on workdays and ornamented bonnets on holidays. The hand-woven skirts could weigh up to six kilograms (13 pounds).

Left:
Sorbs maintain their traditions and customs, such as the artistic way they paint Easter eggs as well as fasting in the weeks before Easter.

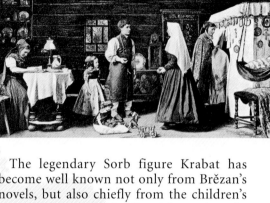

The legendary Sorb figure Krabat has become well known not only from Brězan's novels, but also chiefly from the children's book *Krabat* by Otfried Preussler, written in German. In it, he quite freely alters the substance of the tale of 14-year-old Krabat, a poor boy from Upper Lusatia, who is apprenticed by a miller. Yet, his new master is an evil sorcerer and Krabat almost becomes the victim of black magic. He is saved by the love of his mother and of a maiden. Today, Krabat has been turned into a brand: Krabat the play, the opera and the movie, Krabat beer and herb liqueur; there is even a Krabat bike route in Upper Lusatia in Saxony.

It is not easy for the Sorbs to preserve their autonomy as a people. After the Second World War, industrialization in the power and textiles industries brought many strangers to their ancient homeland. Now, many of their young people must move away, since Lusatia offers them no vocational opportunities. Nevertheless, Lausitz, Łużyca or Lusatia – meaning "marshland" in Sorbian – will remain their home, their "Domowina" where the Sorb anthem sounds: "Lusatia, beautiful land, promise of true friendship! Homeland of my father's joy, lovely vision of my dreams, holy are thy fields to me!"

Above:
...nce, as the devil incar-ate was ploughing the ...d of the Spree, work ...as too slow for him. ...e became angry and ...hipped the oxen until

they jumped in all directions; that is why the Spree is so crooked – according to Sorbian legend. Never mind: Near Burg, the crooked Spree is a lovely sight.

Above right:
This portrayal of a Sorbian farmer's cottage gives the impression of a peaceful, idyllic life. Yet, the daily lives of the Sorbs were characterized by hardship and hard work.

Right:
One thousand years ago, a fortress of the Slavic Luzici tribe stood in Raddusch. Lusatia derived its name from them. This structure, built on the same spot in 2003, imitates the Slavic castle.

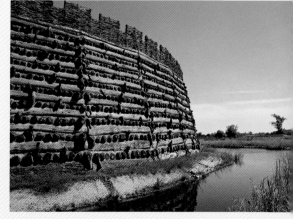

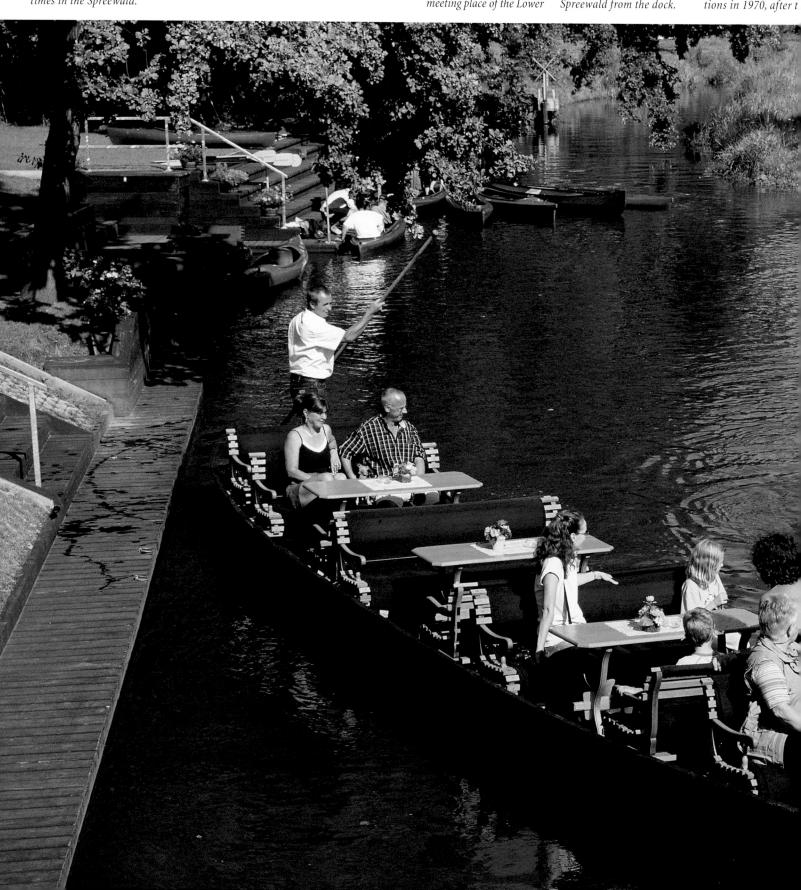

Below:
"Merrily, merrily, merrily, merrily, life is but a dream." – Or so it seems sometimes in the Spreewald.

Above right:
Lübben's heyday is long past: upon passing to Prussia in 1815, "Lubin" lost its importance as the meeting place of the Lower Lusatian landed gentry. Yet, today Lübben is back on top as a tourism magnet. The punts set off to both the lower and upper Spreewald from the dock.

Centre righ
Merely a memory: T Spreewald Station Burg closed down oper tions in 1970, after t

narrow-gauge railway "Spreewaldguste" let off steam for the last time. day, we can still view a few wagons.

Below right:
A quiet spot: Burg in the Spreewald (Sorbian "Borkowy" means "little pine wood").

194 navigable waterways wind through the town, which was once famed for its linen.

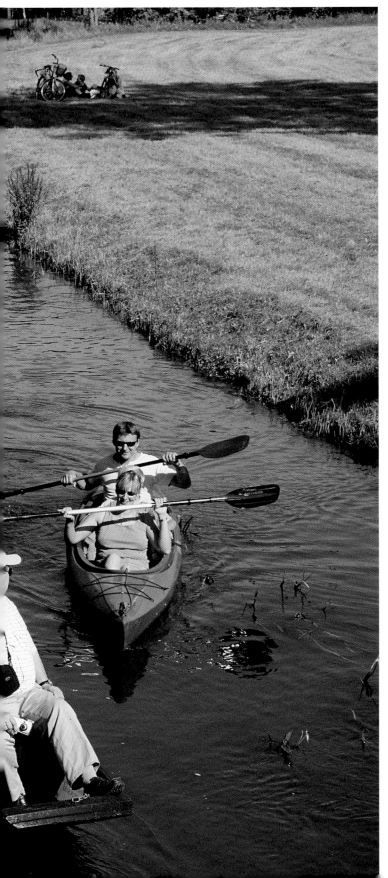

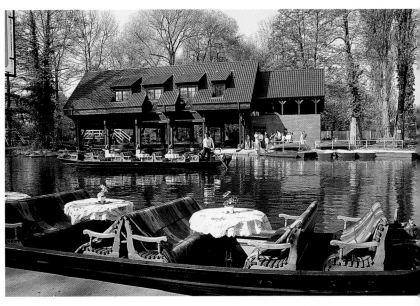

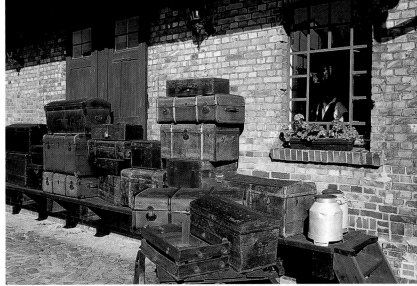

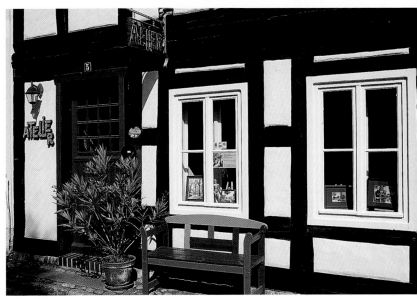

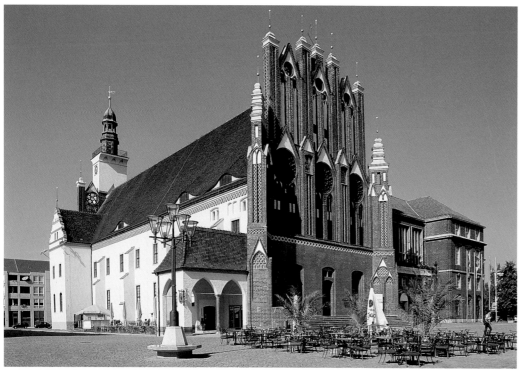

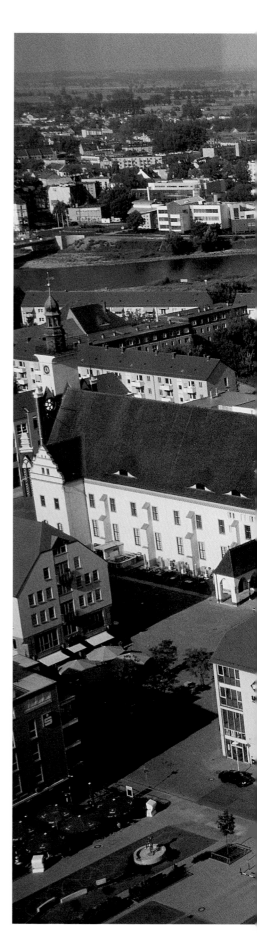

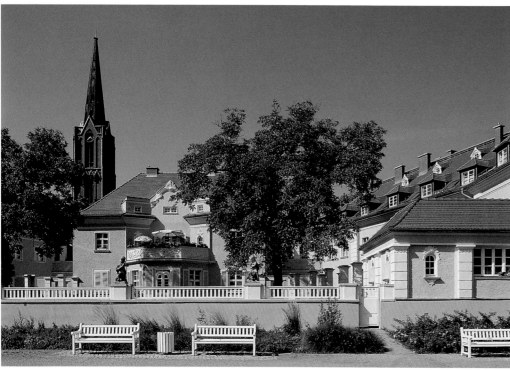

Above:
With its three bridges over the Oder, Frankfurt became the centre of German-Polish relations. The reestablishment of the European University Viadrina in particular is helping to strengthen the relationship with Germany's eastern neighbours.

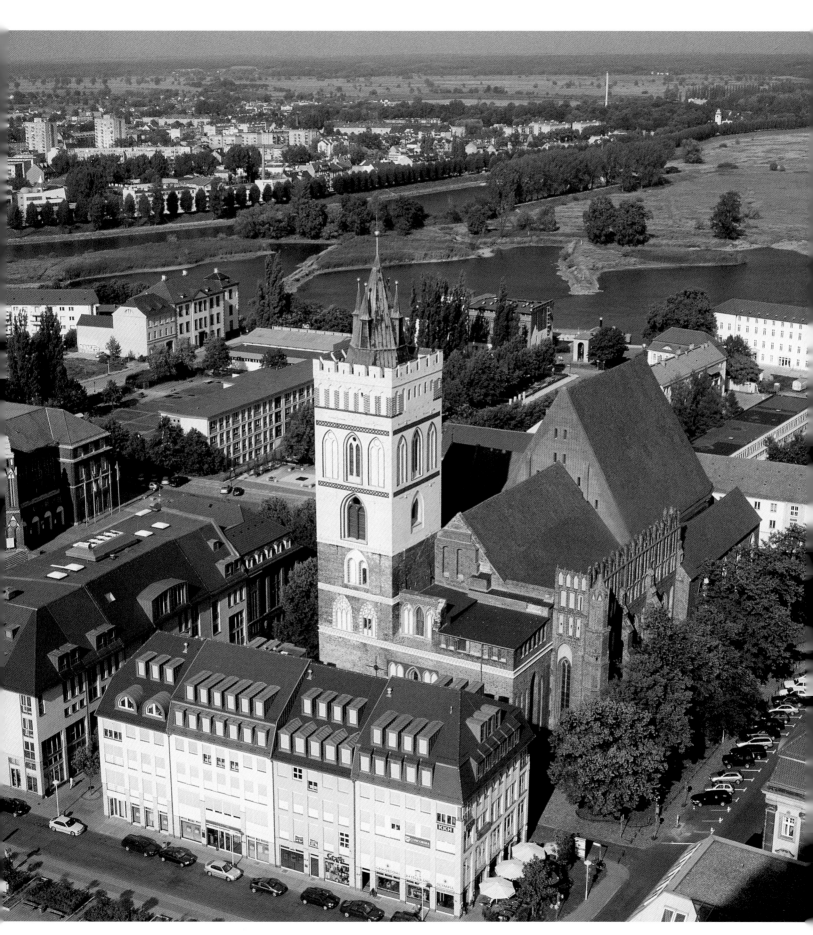

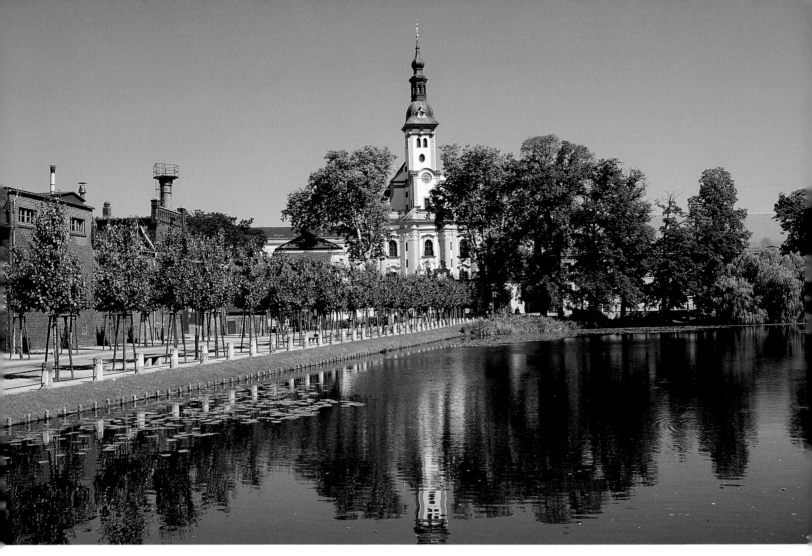

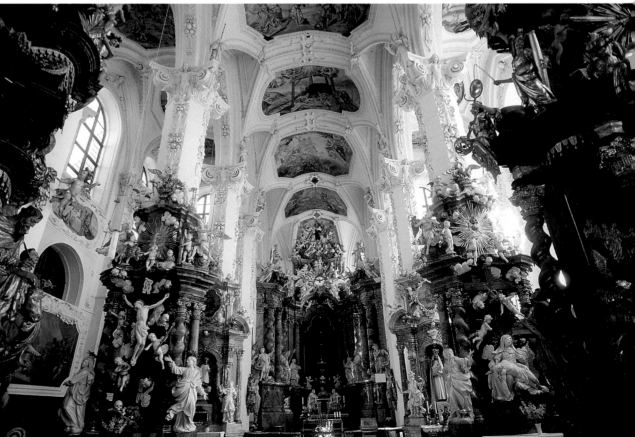

Above:
In the late 13th century, the Cistercians founded a monastery in Neuzelle. The Church of Mary was the victim of a fire in 1429. It was rebuilt in the early 18th century, renovated and expanded in Baroque style.

Right:
Since Neuzelle once was part of Bohemia, its monastery church was the only of Brandenburg to survive the Reformation. Deep Catholicism in Protestant Brandenburg is manifested in lavish Baroque in the stucco ceilings, frescoes, paintings, carvings and décor of all kinds, created by artists from Bohemia, Swabia and Italy.

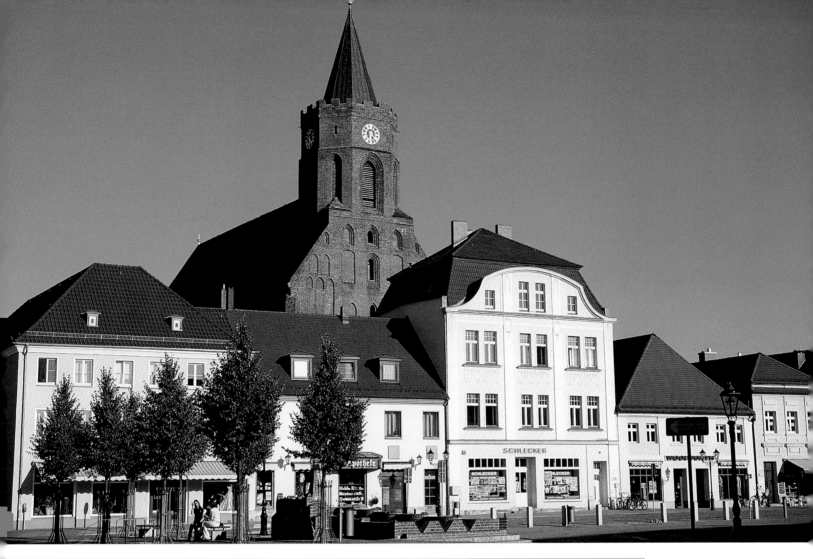

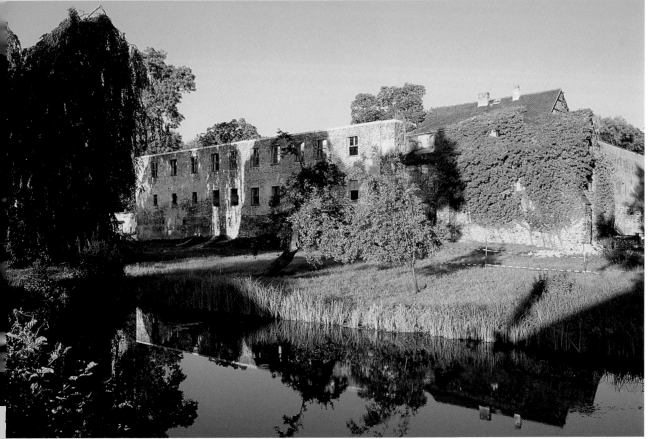

Above:
Beeskow is characterized by a square layout and right-angled streets offering plenty of sights: a castle, a medieval city wall, half-timbered houses and the 14th century Church of Mary. It burnt down in April 1945 and in 2002, its reconstruction was completed with the placement of the spire.

Left:
Castle Storkow, one of the oldest and most significant castles of eastern Brandenburg. The ravages of time have left their mark on it since the 14th century until, in 1978, the main building burnt down entirely. Reconstruction began in 1998 and the aim of future use is to create an internationally sophisticated attraction.

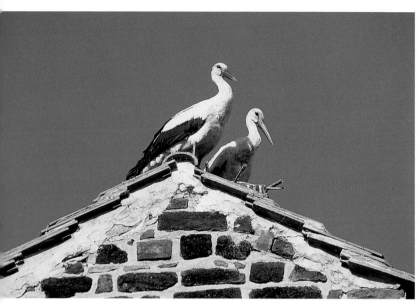

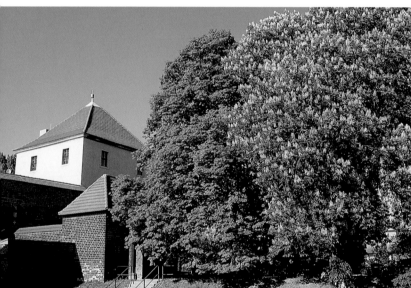

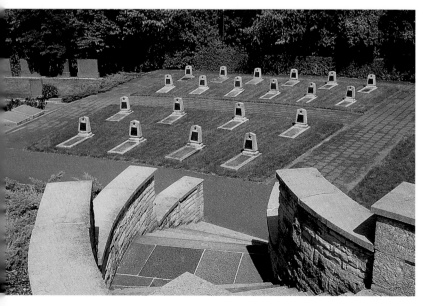

*Above left
and centre:*

*Above left
and centre:*
For over two centuries,
castle Friedland in the
little town of the same

name was the seat of
the Order of St. John of
Jerusalem. Storks nest on
the roof ridge of the imposing castle of the order.

Below left:
The Seelow Heights
memorial commemorat
the largest battle of the
Second World War on
German soil. In the win
ter and spring of 1945,

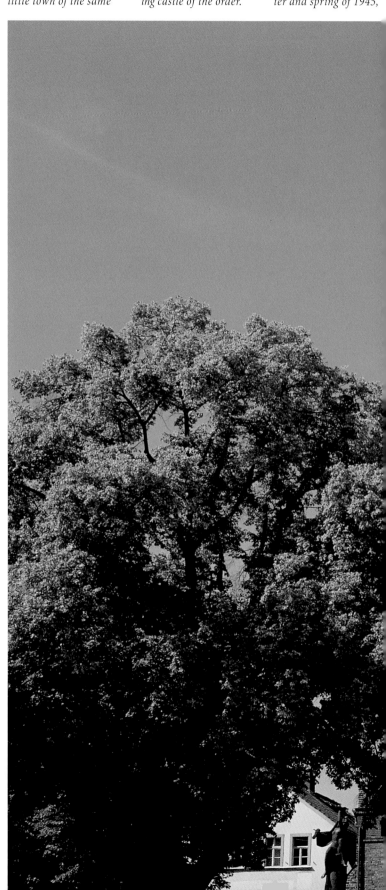

ore than one hundred ousand soldiers of any nationalities died the fight for the bridge-eads and the battle r the Seelow Heights.

Former German president Richard von Weizsäcker warned: "Whoever refuses to remember the inhumanity is prone to new risks of infection."

Below:
Bad Freienwalde is the oldest health resort in the Mark Brandenburg. The little town surrounding the church of St. Nikolai

radiates provincial charm. The palace and a few villas tell of the good old days when kings recuperated here. Walther Rathenau,

foreign minister of the German Empire in 1922, lived here for many years. A memorial commemorates his eventful life.

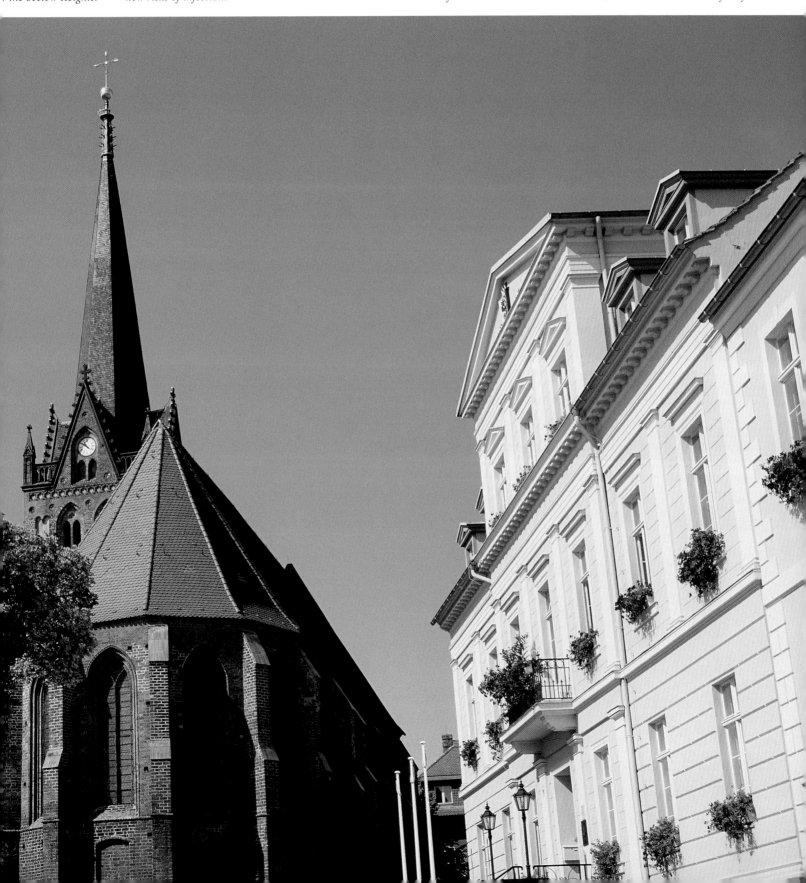

"Majesty, in Buckow the lungs walk on velvet!" are the words used by Frederick William IV's personal physician to recommend the climatic and spa health resort on Lake Schermützel. Buckow and the Märkische Schweiz nature park offer the best prerequisites for restful recreation. Even playwright Bertolt Brecht, who enjoyed this view from his summer cottage, appreciated it.

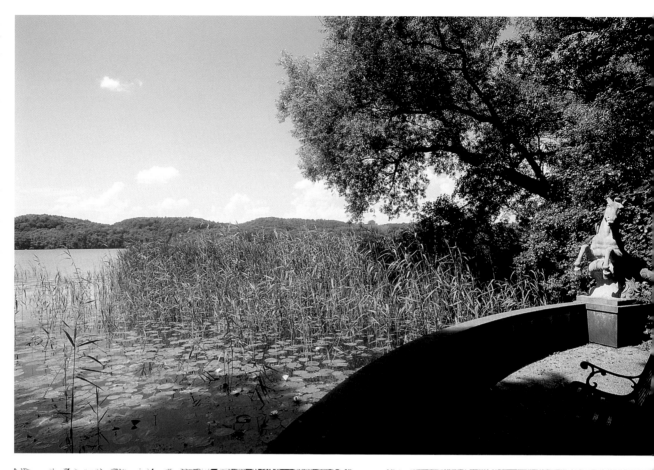

The walking path around Lake Schermützel – the largest lake in the Märkische Schweiz – offers many opportunities to stop and rest and all of them include a free lovely view.

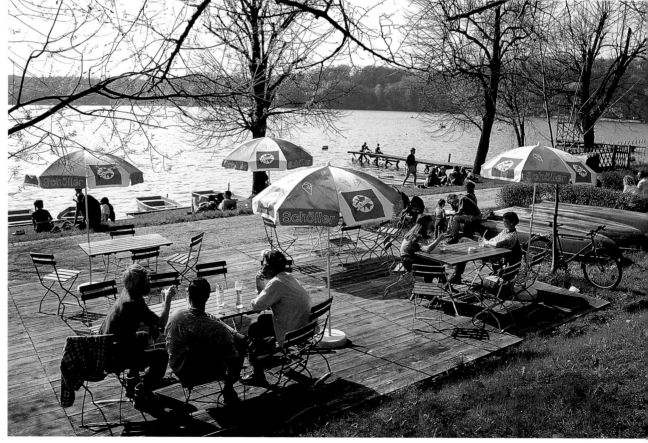

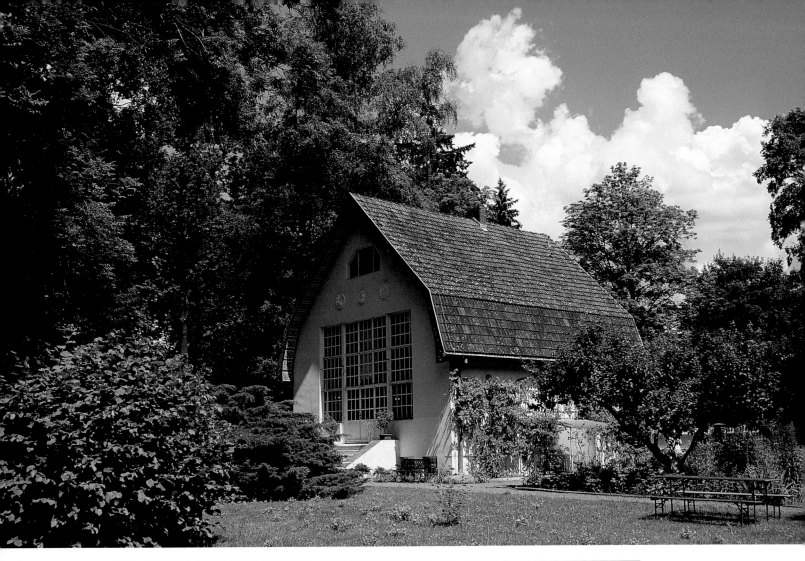

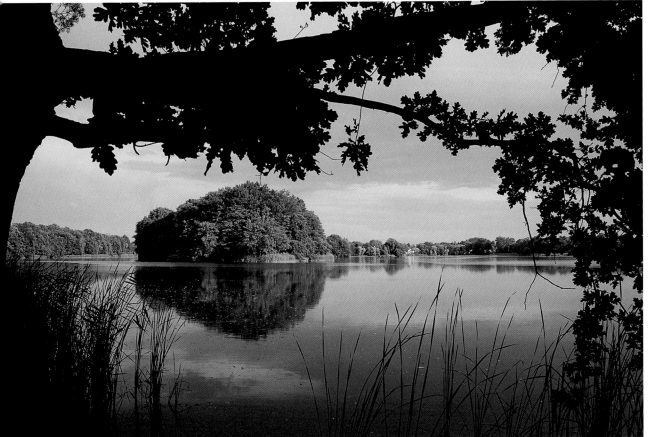

Above:
Here, in the summer cottage of Bert Brecht and Helene Weigel, the "Buckow Elegies" were written. The cycle of works is introduced with these laconic four lines: "If a breeze blew there / I could set a sail / If I had no sail / I would make one of sticks and canvas."

Left:
"There are roads and villages meant for driving through and there are those that invite one to stay, and it has something to do with the trees." (Günter de Bruyn) Obersdorf in the Märkische Schweiz invites you to stay …

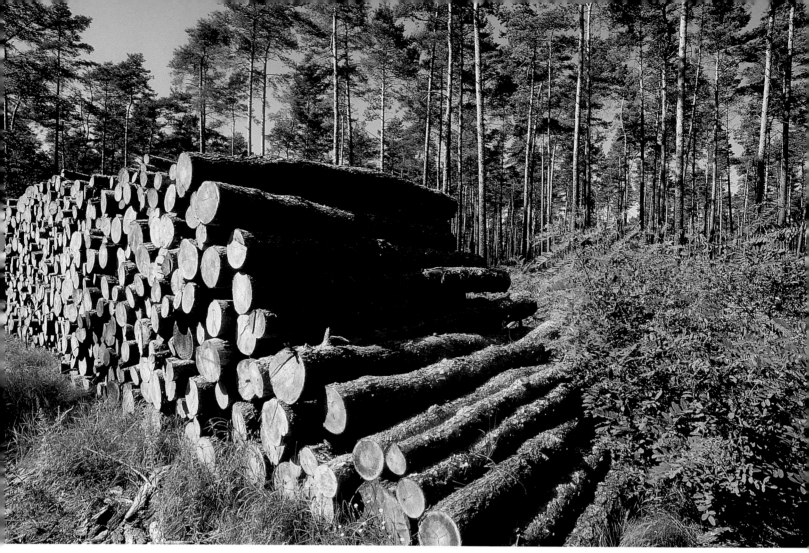

Above:
Wood near Treppeln in the Märkische Schweiz. Compared to the other villages of the district, the town has the largest area of forest on its terrain. In 1994, it was named the most beautiful village of the entire rural district of Oder-Spree.

Right:
The church of Münchehofe, "monks' courtyard," is a structure of hewn boulders from the second half of the 13th century. It houses a Late Gothic winged altarpiece dating from about 1520.

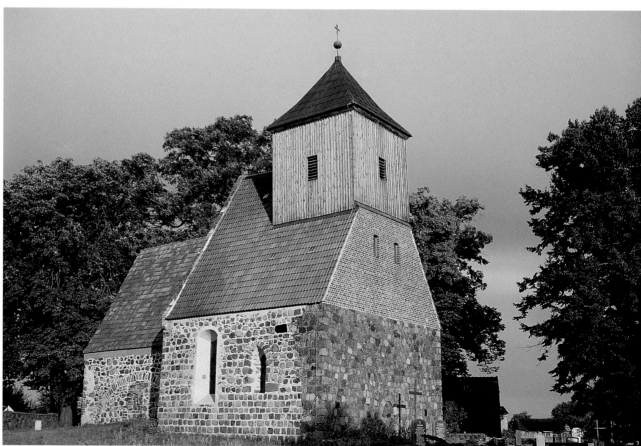

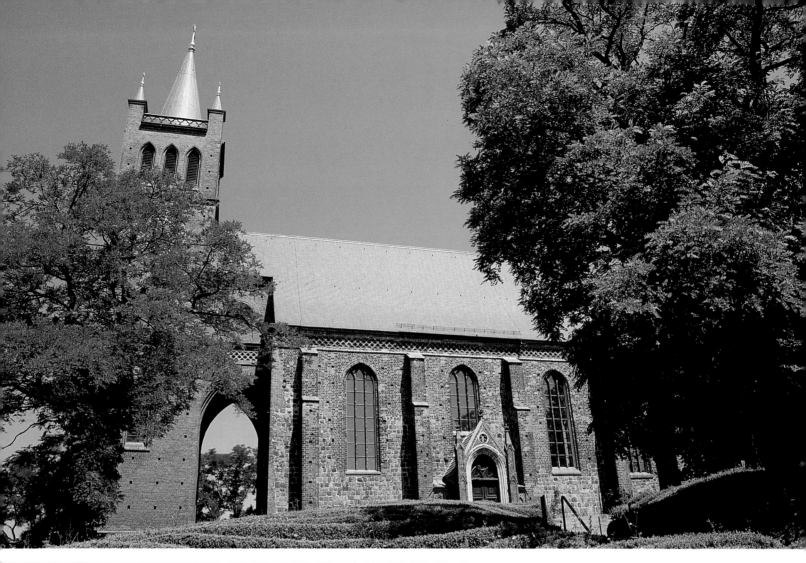

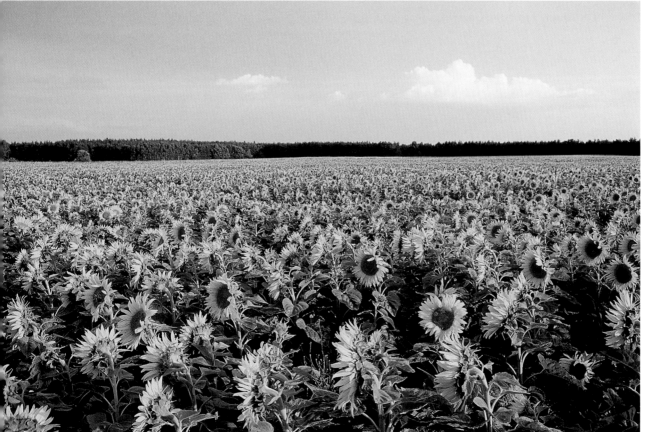

Above:
The Müncheberger parish church of St. Mary was erected on the remains of a medieval granite wall. Its tower was designed by Karl Friedrich Schinkel. It is connected to the nave by an open narthex with a high pointed arch.

Left:
Like a sea of gold: sunflower fields by Münchehofe.

Below:
Over the centuries, castle
Wulkow has had many
owners. In GDR times,
the building was used
as a hospital, as a refugee

home and a combine
training school. Its
purchase by an investor
saved it from ruin; it has
been operated as a hotel
since 1994.

Above right:
The many tree-lined
avenues of his
Brandenburg homeland
once moved the writer
Erwin Strittmatter to
this philosophical reflection: "Now and again, the

earth dwellers we c▢
trees parade their d▢
tinctiveness especia▢
clearly. It depends on t▢
position of the light. Y▢
the light depends on t▢
season, the season on t▢

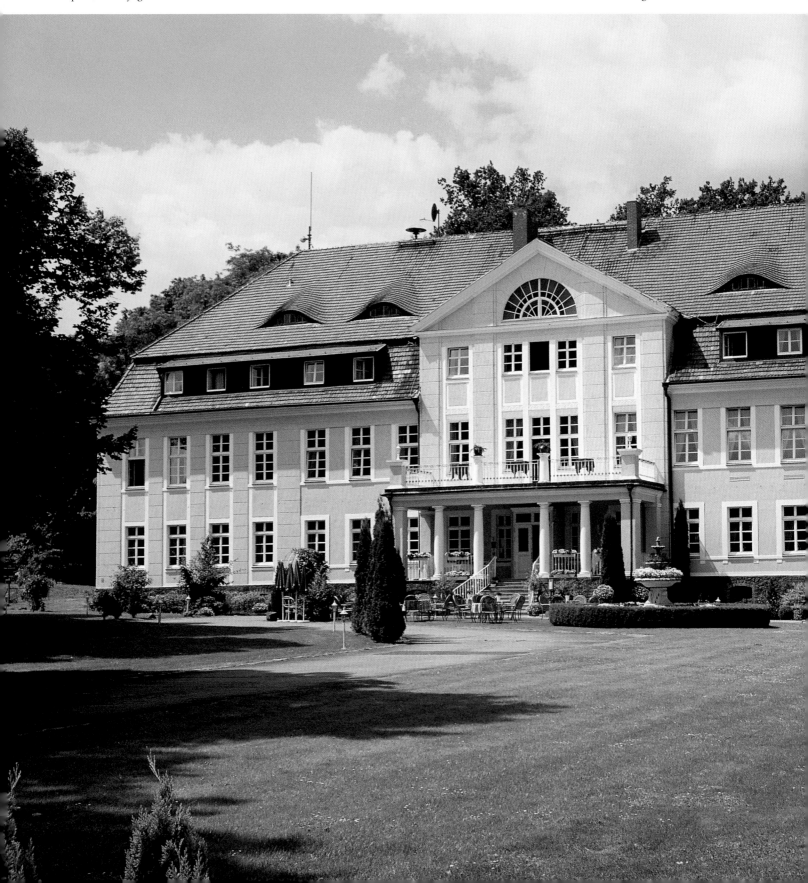

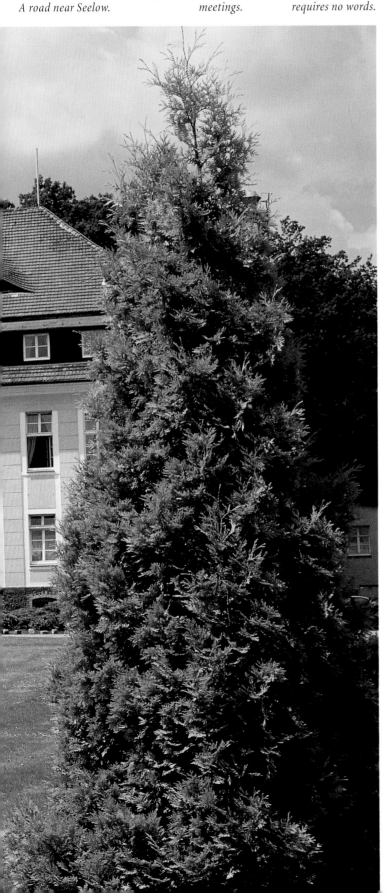

position of the earth and the position of the earth on the changing conditions in the universe: ence all things on earth have their time." – A road near Seelow.

Centre right:
The Lenné gardens of Neuhardenberg Palace. In 2003 and 2004, the cabinet of the German government retreated to this idyllic site for private meetings.

Below right:
Near Ketzin: pure nature – a symphony that requires no words.

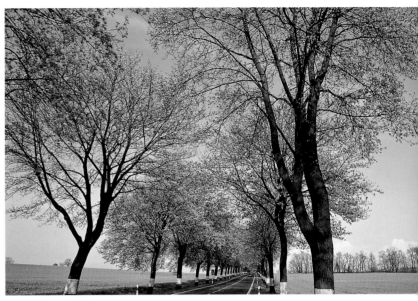

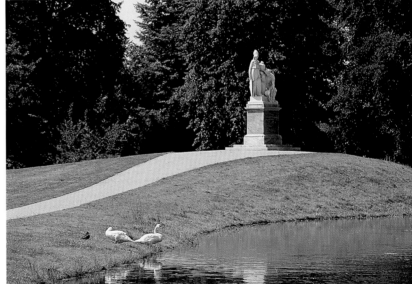

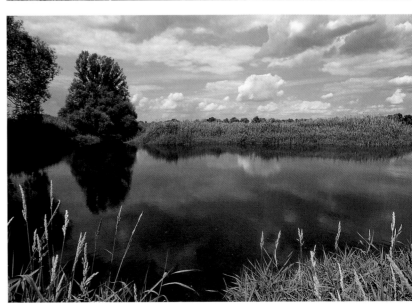

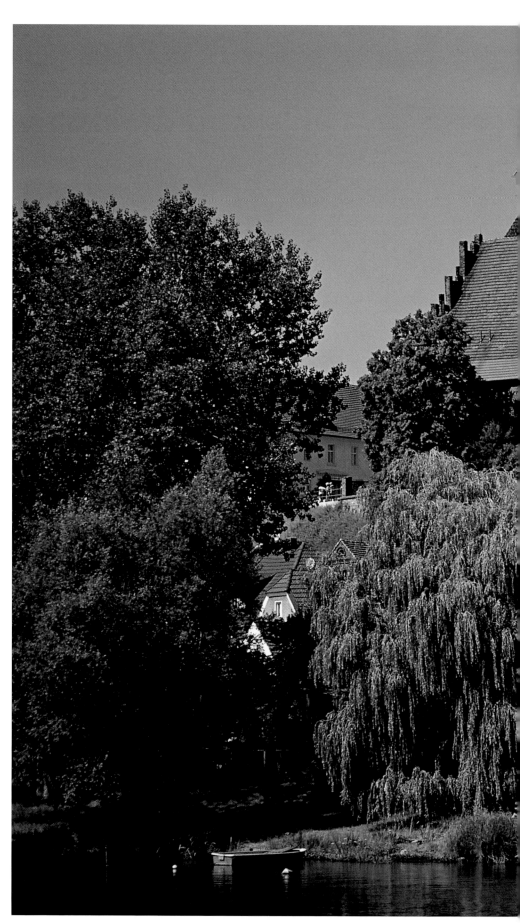

Havelberg calls itself the "island and cathedral town in the green." The small town with a big past – in the Middle Ages it was a bishopric – lies picturesquely on a pen-insula in the river Havel. When exploring the north-west of Brandenburg, a side trip to Havelberg is a treat, even though the town has been part of the state of Saxony-Anhalt since reunification.

The gently rolling landscapes of Prignitz, Ruppiner Land and Uckermark in the north of Brandenburg were shaped by terminal moraines in the Ice Age. Nature reserves, national parks and biosphere reserves have been established to preserve their natural harmony. The parks are the frequent homes of cranes, herons and storks.

Frederick the Great as well had a temporary home in Rheinsberg – as a prince before he himself became king. The little Rococo palace was a gift from his father. In 1740, he wrote, "We dance till out of breath and eat till full to bursting." Much later, Kurt Tucholsky enjoyed himself in this town and there he wrote in 1912 his novel *Rheinsberg: A Picture Book for Lovers.*

At the sewing machine factory in Wittenberge stands a curiosity: Germany's highest tower clock dating from 1903. In 1636, Wittstock, a former bishopric, was the scene of a dreadful battle of the Thirty Years' War that was won by the Swedes. A museum in the tower of the old bishop's palace is a memorial to this long, brutal conflict in the heart of Europe.

You can experience the ambience of past centuries in Oranienburg or Perleberg, in Neuruppin or Schwedt: magnificent churches and town halls, imposing squares, mighty city walls, powder magazines and old gates. In 1530 in Angermünde, merchant Hans Kohlhase bought two horses that were stolen from him in 1532 on the way to the Leipzig fair. For years, he fought in vain for his rights until himself turning criminal; he was executed in 1540. Heinrich von Kleist erected a literary memorial to this man with his novella *Michael Kohlhaas.*

Templin, the "Pearl of Uckermark" now has a new claim to fame: Angela Merkel, the first female chancellor of the Federal Republic of Germany, grew up here.

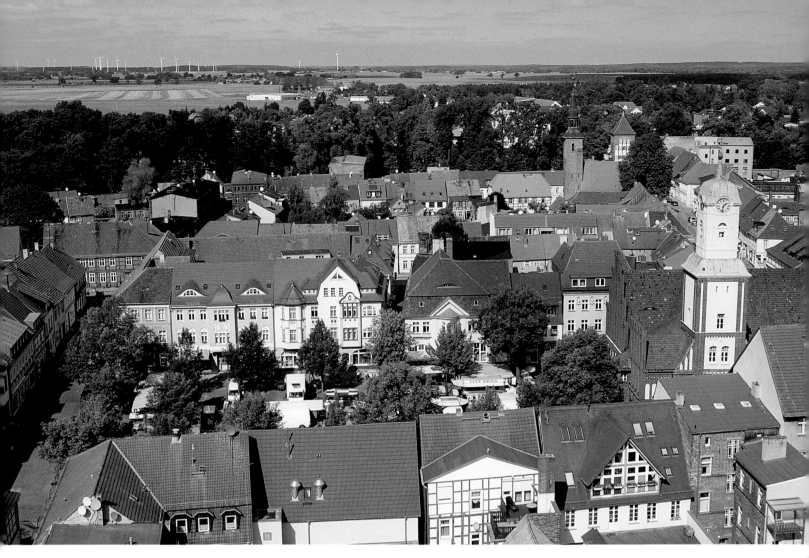

Above:
In 1636, one of the bloodiest battles of the Thirty Years' War took place before the gates of Wittstock, as a Swedish army fought imperial and Saxon troops. A witness, Johann Jakob Christoffel von Grimmelshausen, wrote of the battle in his Simplicissimus: "The earth, accustomed to covering the dead, was then at this place itself covered by the dead, each bearing their own marks, there lay heads that had lost their natural lords and here lay bodies lacking heads…"

Right:
The large market square of Wittstock, one of the oldest cities east of the Elbe, is dominated by a Neo-Gothic town hall and adjacent courthouse portico.

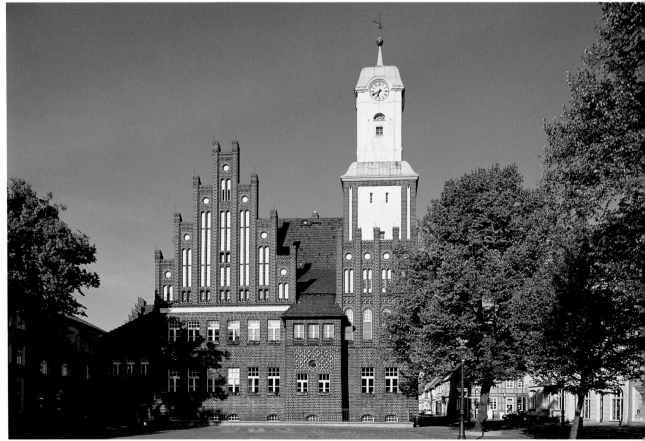

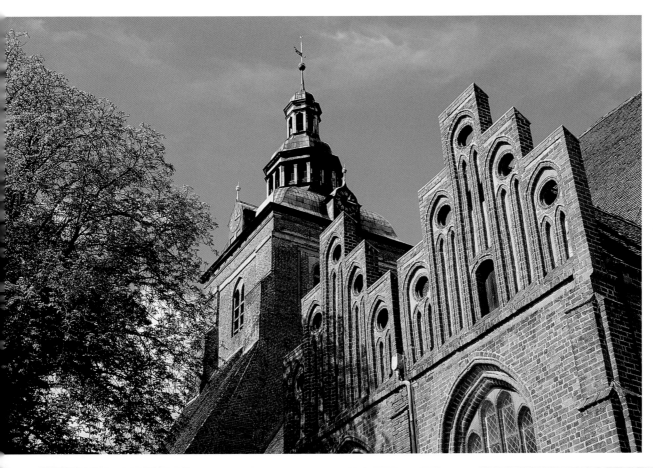

Left:
Wittstock is also known as the "Rothenburg of the march." Half-timbered houses on narrow, bumpy cobblestone streets and crooked alleys are part of the town's special charm. The city church of St. Mary with its high tower, visible from miles away, is one of the finest features. Construction of the church began in the 13th century.

Below:
The coronation of Mary is not mentioned in the Bible, yet the ideal of the royal majesty of Jesus' Mother was part of the Christian faith in the Middle Ages. The Neo-Gothic carved altar, made by the Lübeck artist Claus Berg, illustrates the event.

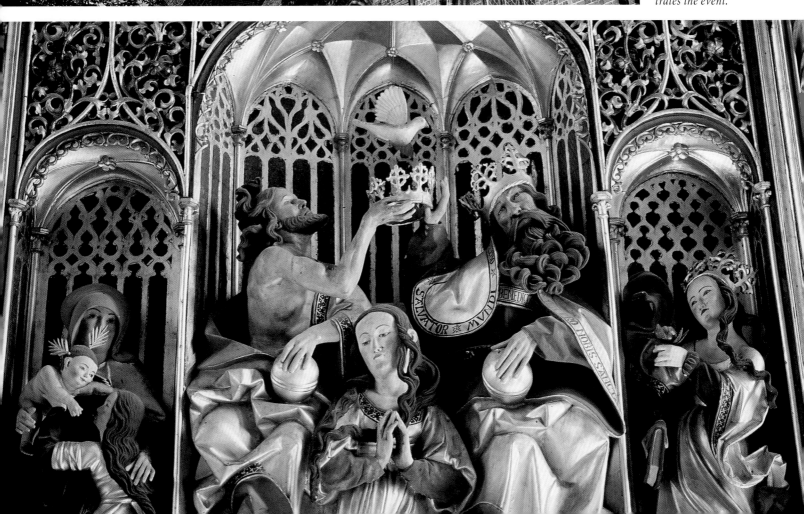

In the 14th century, in the days when the little river of Stepenitz was still navigable and formed a link to the Elbe, Perleberg became a member of the Hanseatic League and one of the wealthiest cities of the Mark Brandenburg. The town hall was built during the town's heyday; but the brick gable was not added until 1839.

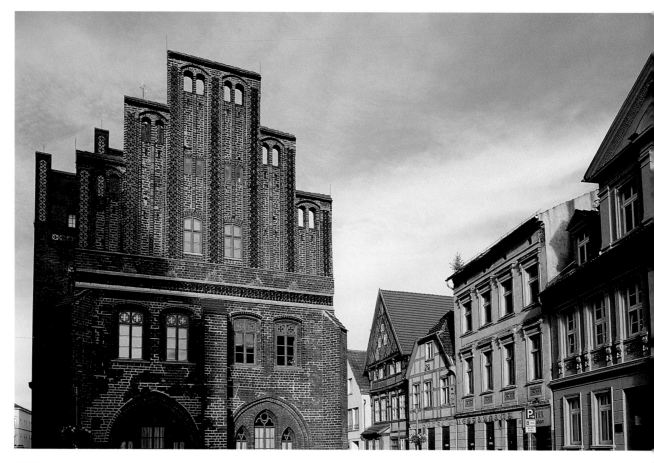

The market square with its fortress-like town hall, a brick structure dating from 1879, forms the heart of the city of Kyritz. A Bible from the 15th century is exhibited in the meeting hall – translated into Lower German even before Martin Luther. A nice little town that made its way into the history books even in the GDR: it was from here that Wilhelm Pieck announced the land reform in 1945. According to legend, the clattering of its mills gave the town the middle name "on the Knatter."

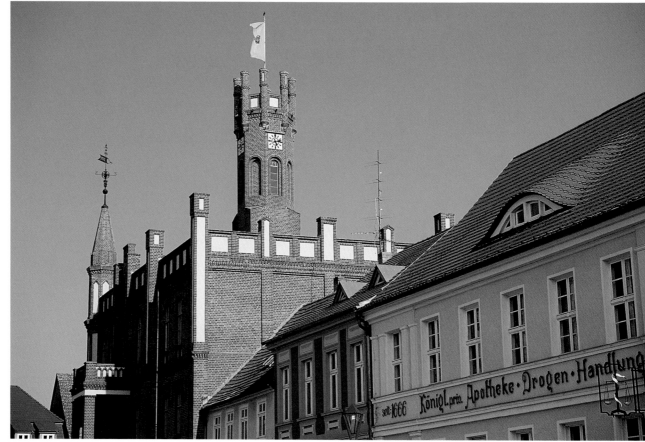

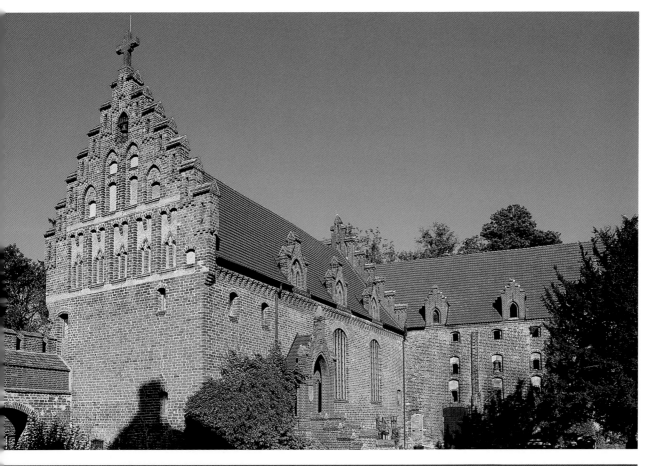

The Plattenburg in Bad Wilsnack is the oldest preserved moated castle of northern Germany. Surrounded by embankments and double moats, the castle served as a summer residence for the bishops of Havelberg from 1319 until 1548. Every summer, the Plattenburg invites one and all to a medieval spectacle.

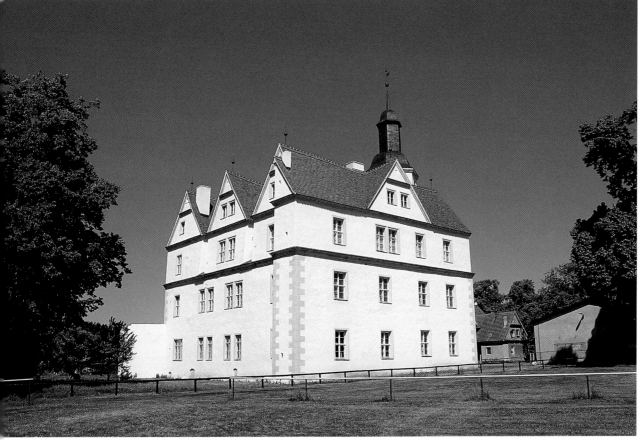

The castle of Demerthin displays the typical shape of country manor houses from before the Thirty Years' War. The peculiar structure with the three closely grouped gables was intended to make the essentially plain building look more magnificent.

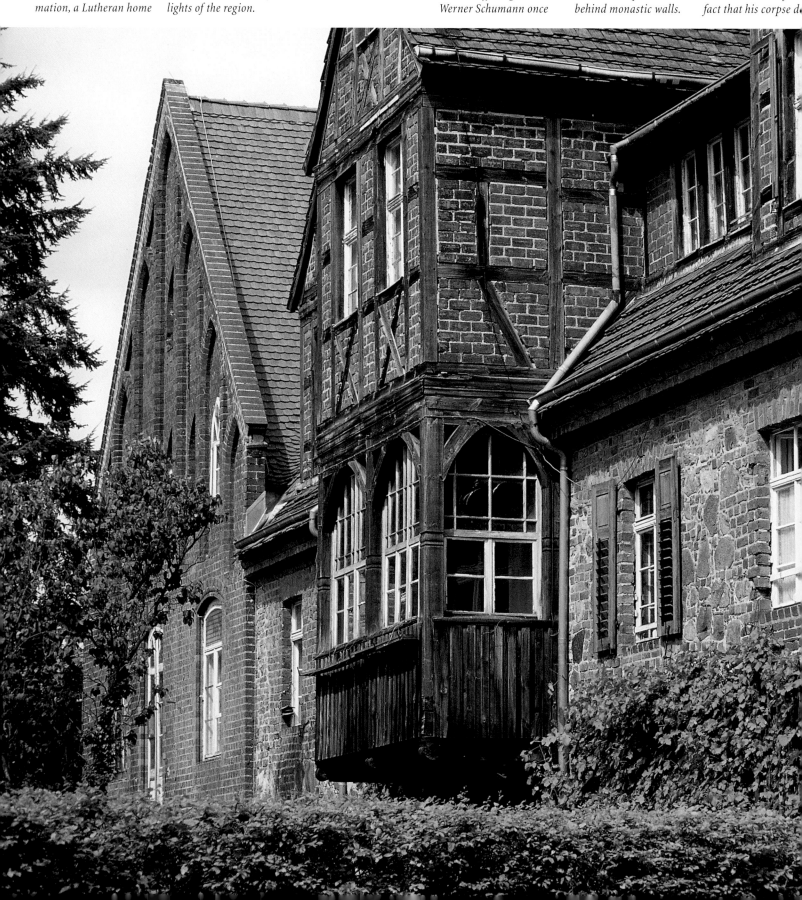

Below:
Close to Wittstock lies Heiligengrabe, a former convent from the Middle Ages. After the Reformation, a Lutheran home for elderly gentlewomen was established here. – The summer concerts are among the cultural highlights of the region.

Above right:
World history left them standing as "symbols of slow consolidation in a sea of unrest and suffering," wrote Werner Schumann once of Heiligengrabe and the march's other monasteries and convents. After centuries, the structures still fulfil their purpose: to create a small, quiet world behind monastic walls.

**Centre rig
and belo**
The mortuary chapel
Kampehl shelters a fame
body: Sir Kahlbutz.
was not honoured for
saintliness, but for
fact that his corpse d

ot decompose. The aristocratic bad boy died in 702 at the young age of 1 years. Beforehand, he made himself unpopular the region by claiming he right to deflower the brides in his dominion on their wedding nights. It is said that he had thirty illegitimate children in addition to his eleven legitimate children. Famous physicians such as Virchow and Sauerbruch examined the mummy, ascertained that it had not been embalmed, and hence the riddle of Sir Kahlbutz remains unsolved.

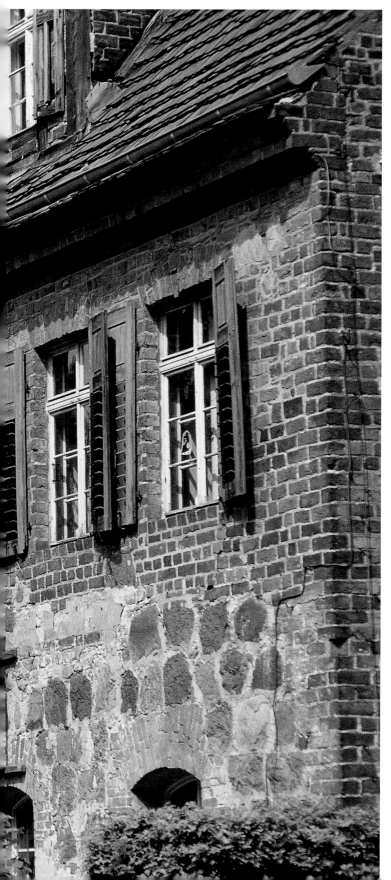

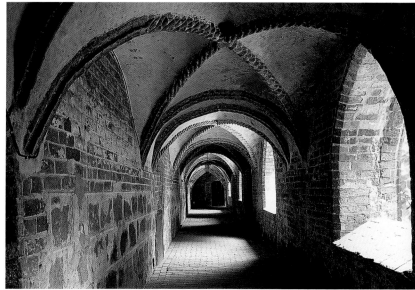

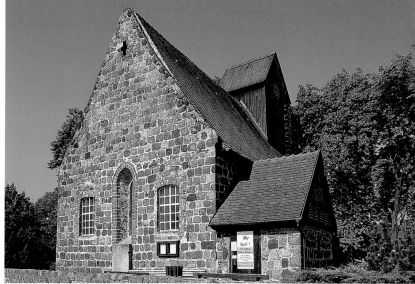

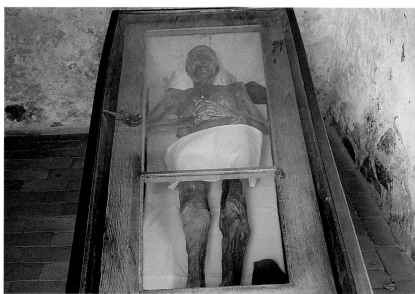

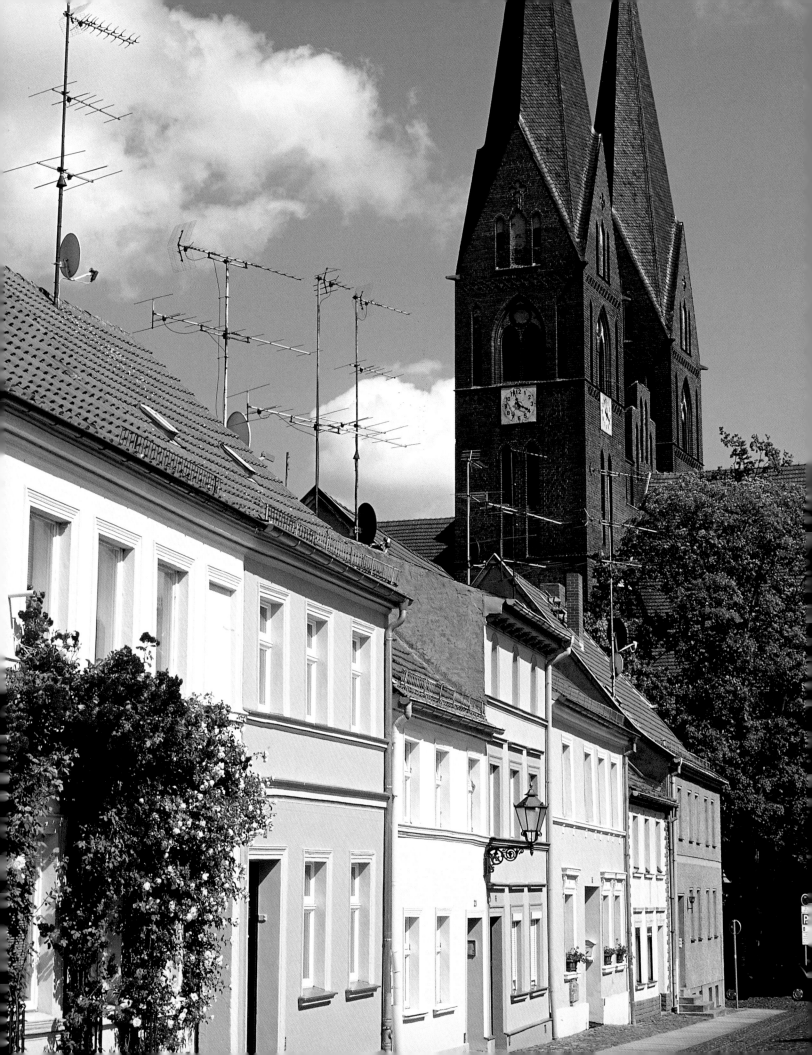

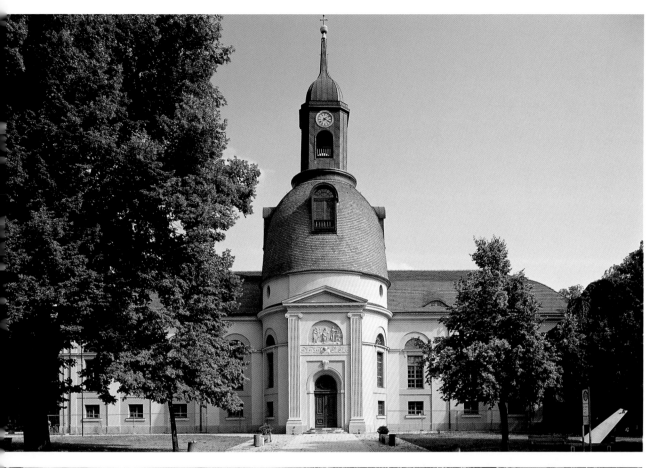

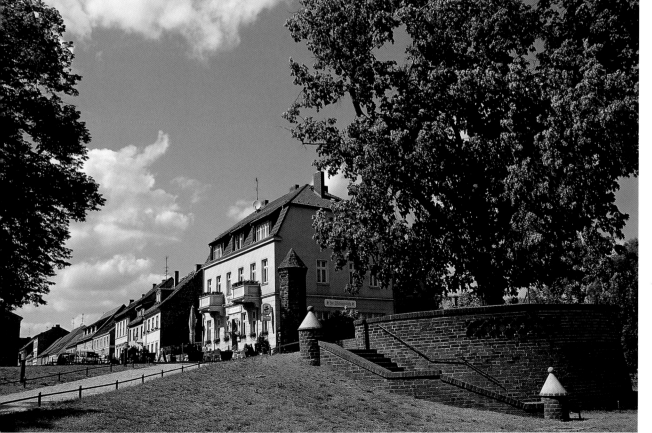

The former parish church of St. Mary in Neuruppin is an unusual structure; the transept is entered from the middle of the long side. In 1806, the house of worship was dedicated after being rebuilt following the fire of 1787. Today, the church is no longer used for sacred purposes, but as a cultural and congress centre.

Left-hand page:
Neuruppin presents itself properly to its guests from near and far, who visit the hometown of such famous men as Schinkel and Fontane. The poet once scoffed that the most irregular things in Neuruppin were the irregular Latin verbs he had to learn ... The Protestant Trinity Church goes back to the 13th century; the decorative twin steeples were not added until 1906-1907.

Wichmann von Arnstein was the name of the first prior of the former Dominican monastery in Neuruppin. Many legends are told of the monk's life, not only during the traditional Wichmann Festival. The age of the magnificent lime tree is estimated at 700 years. They say a treasure is buried beneath it.

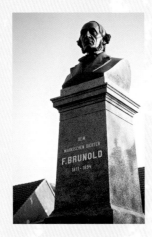

In his day, the teacher August Ferdinand Meyer (1811–1894) became an esteemed homeland poet of the Werbellin landscape under the pseudonym Friedrich Brunold. This bronze monument in Joachimsthal was set up in his honour.

There is a common German adage *"Das ist ein weites Feld"* meaning "that's too vast a subject" that was coined by a character in the novel *Effi Briest* by Theodor Fontane (1819–1898) whom Kurt Tucholsky called the "Goethe of the march." On 30 December 1819, he was born in Neuruppin, where his father ran a pharmacy. In Berlin, he was trained in his

as we read in the foreword, some landscape, some history, tales of customs and of characters. The Rambles formed the foundation for his great novels, such as *Effi Briest* (1895) and *The Stechlin* (1899).

Authors like Friedrich de la Motte Fouqué (1777–1843), Gerhart Hauptmann (1862–1946) and Georg Kaiser (1878–1945) lived and worked in the Mark Brandenburg, as did Prussia's art-loving King Frederick the Great, who wrote poetry and called the poet-philosopher Voltaire to his court in 1750. Other aristocrats, as well, took up the pen, for example the gardener-artist, adventurer and travel writer Prince Hermann von Pückler-Muskau (1785–1871), the "green prince."

The storyteller and playwright Heinrich von Kleist (1777–1811) was born in Frankfurt an der Oder (*The Broken Pitcher*). Most of the characters in the novels of Willibald Alexis (1798–1871) are natives of Brandenburg. The town of Lehnin, the scene of his most famous novel, *The Trousers of the Lord*

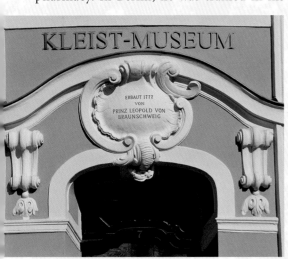

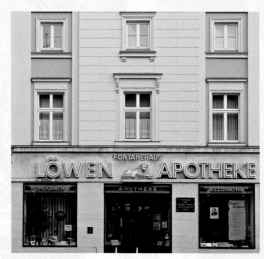

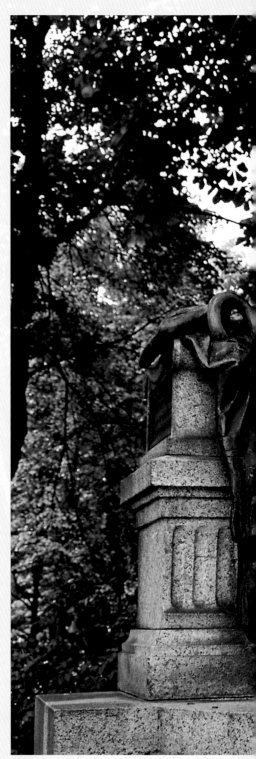

father's vocation, yet already began writing while in training. He actually began his literary career in 1848 as a foreign correspondent in England. During his years there, he wrote a number of books on English life, such as *A Summer in London* (1854) and *Across the Tweed: A Tour of Mid-Victorian Scotland* (1860). His next travel account was based on his homeland: *Rambles through the Mark Brandenburg*, which aided him in his breakthrough as a writer. The work of approximately 3,000 pages, published between 1862 and 1889, was the fruit of thirty years of travels. Fontane explored the march in 113 expeditions via carriage, railway and barge. In a loose, narrative style, he offers,

of Bredow, built a monument to him. The town of Biesenbrow brought forth Ehm Welk (1884–1966), creator of the *Heathens of Kummerow*, for which Biesenbrow stood model.

As a child, Peter Huchel (1903–1981) moved from Berlin to live with his grandparents in Alt-Langerwisch. He became one of Brandenburg's most famous voices. His dark verses are ambiguous, painting a picture of the blood-soaked earth of the region. By contrast, Günter de Bruyn (born in 1926) deals cheerfully with East German literature in his *Märkischen Forschungen* and not coincidently makes the poets' land of Branden-

Above far left:
Walk through the lovely portal of the Kleist Museum in Frankfurt an der Oder to learn everything important about the life and work of the great poet in a lavish exhibition.

Above left:
Still open today: Löwen Apotheke in Neuruppin. On 30 December 1819, Theodor Fontane was born in this house; in hi day, he found the small town bleak and subdue

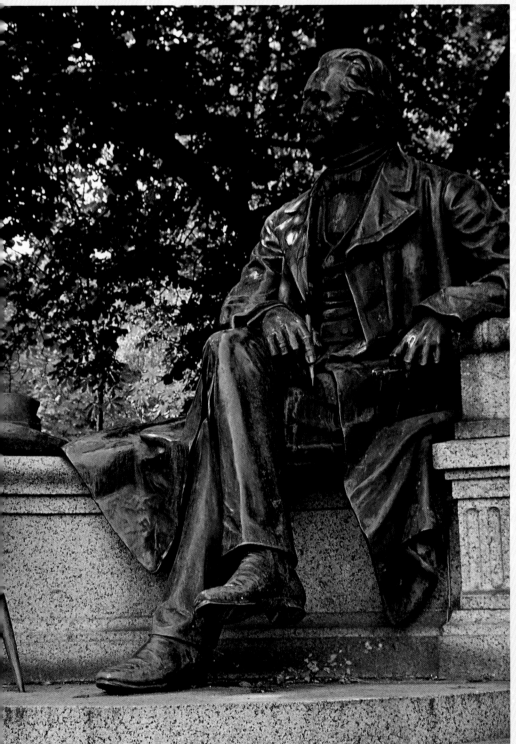

burg the setting of the commotion about the (fictional) poet Max Swedenow. The creator of the trilogy *Der Laden*, Erwin Strittmatter (1912–1994), was born in Bohsdorf in the Lower Lusatia.

HOLIDAY SPOT FOR AUTHORS

Achim von Arnim (1781–1831) and his wife Bettina von Arnim, nee Brentano (1785–1859) made the Baroque palace in Wiepersdorf (Fläming) their new home. Their graves are in the palace gardens. The house later served as a holiday home for the East German writers' society, visited for example by the famed authors Anna Seghers and Arnold Zweig. A similar institution was located on Lake Schwielow until 1990, the "Friedrich Wolf Writers' Holiday Home," previously the residence of actress Marika Rökk. Christa and Gerhard Wolf, Rainer Kunze, Maxie and Fred Wander, Sarah and Rainer Kirsch and many others spent their holidays there.

Other literary greats enjoyed nature in the march in their holiday cottages, like Johannes R. Becher (1891–1958), lyricist of the national anthem of East Germany (1949), in Bad Saarow on Lake Scharmützel. In 1952, Bertolt Brecht and Helene Weigel purchased a summerhouse in Buckow on Lake Schermützel (easily confused with Lake Scharmützel) and immortalized the town in his *Buckow Elegies*.

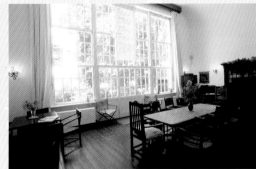

bove:
Observing things means almost more to me than wning them," Fontane *nce said. His monument*

in Neuruppin gives us the impression that he is still observing the world to collect material for new stories.

Above right:
In 1952, the artist couple Bertolt Brecht and Helene Weigel purchased a house in Buckow on Lake Schermützel "on a lovely lot by the water … under old, big trees," as the playwright noted in his work journal.

Right:
A pear tree made it famous, the cemetery at Ribbeck in the Havelland. Many generations of children learned Theodor Fontane's poem by heart at school.

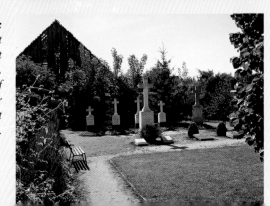

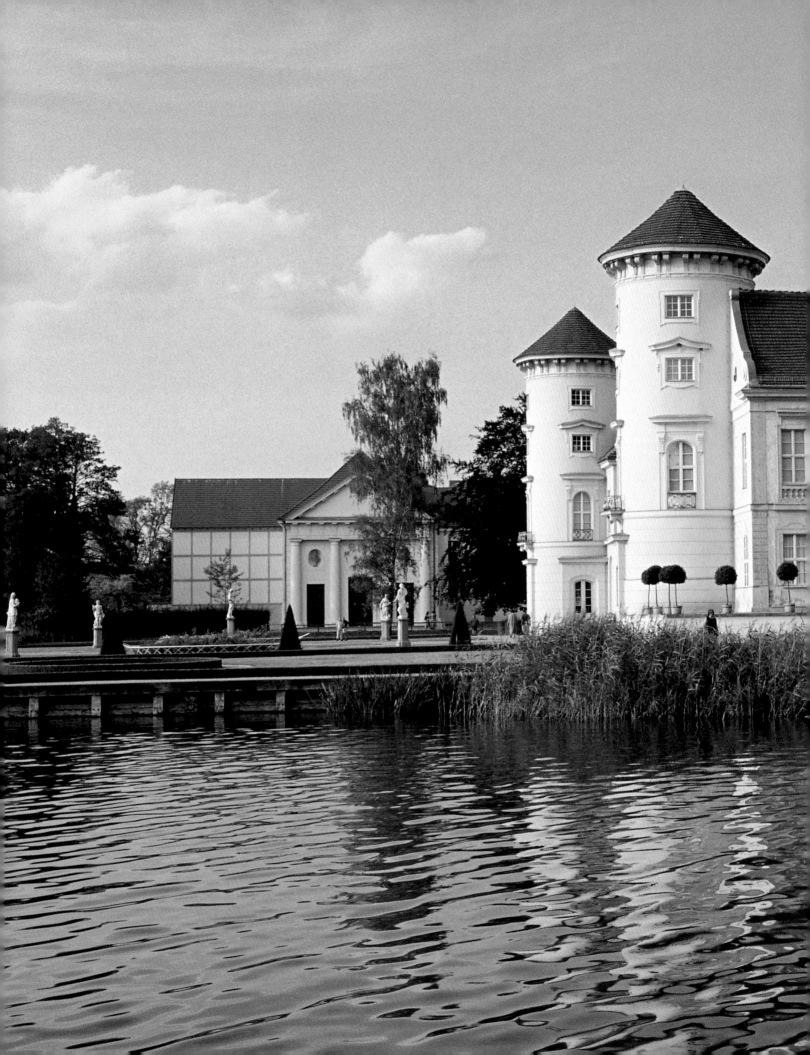

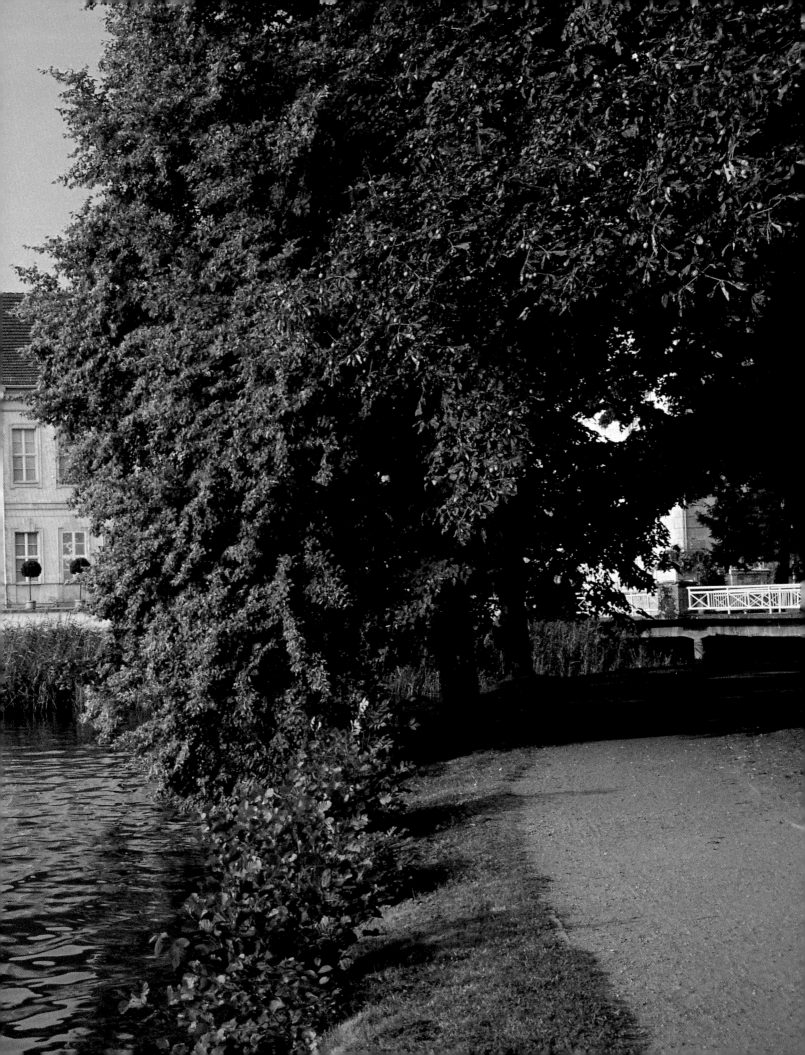

"Meadows, water and sand: that is the march land!" says an old song. Ingredients that make Brandenburg so attractive, like here near Wuthenow on the shore of Lake Ruppin.

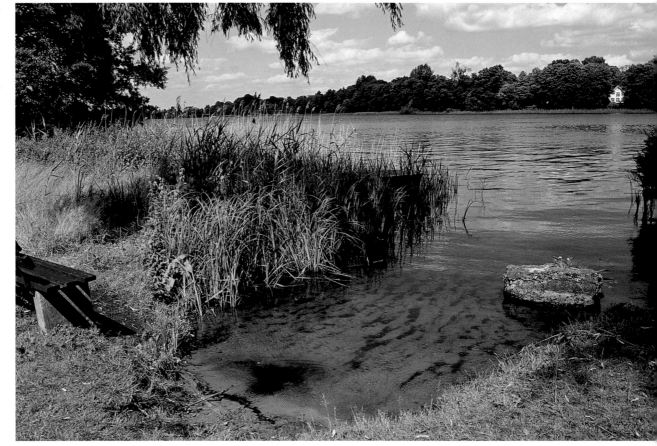

Pages 104/105:
Crown Prince Frederick lived in Rheinsberg Palace before becoming "the Great" as king. A former castle, rebuilt in the Renaissance style, unfolded its splendour through the star architect Knobelsdorff in "Frederickan Rococo." Frederick spent his leisure time here enjoying music, literature and philosophy. Kurt Tucholsky wrote his A Picture Book for Lovers in Rheinsberg. Even today, the traveller senses the special magic of this lovely place.

Little Fürstenberg has a special treasure: The Protestant town church is built of yellow brick erected by Schinkel's student Friedrich Wilhelm Buttel from 1845 to 1848 in the Neo-Byzantine style. It contains Europe's largest batik tapestry, showing the resurrection of Christ.

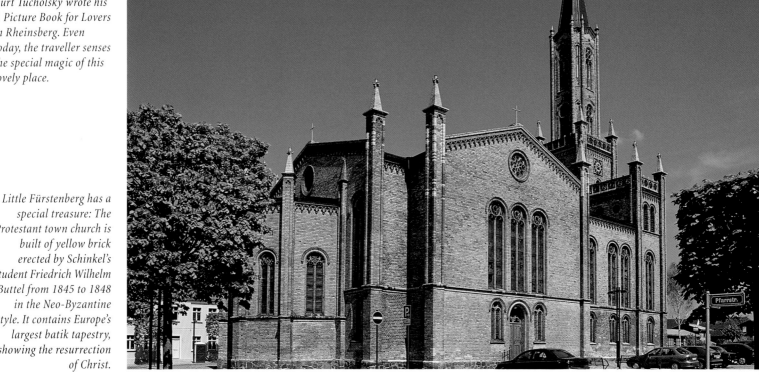

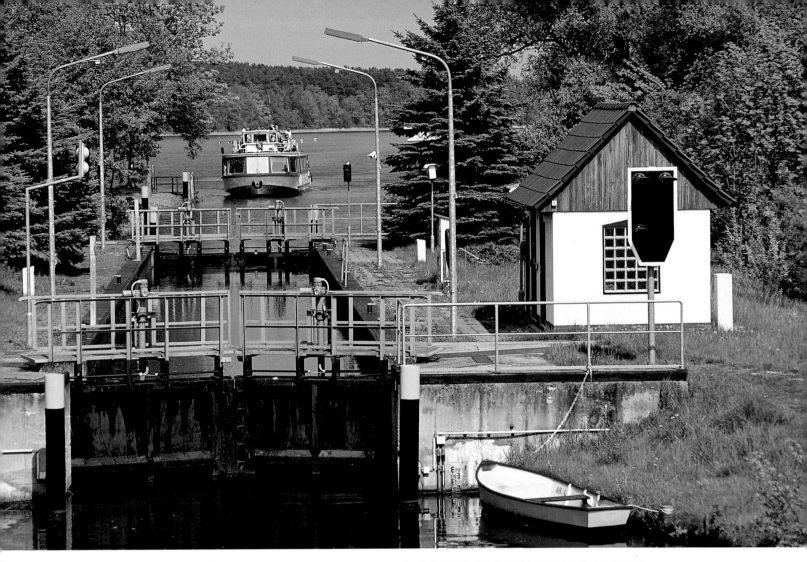

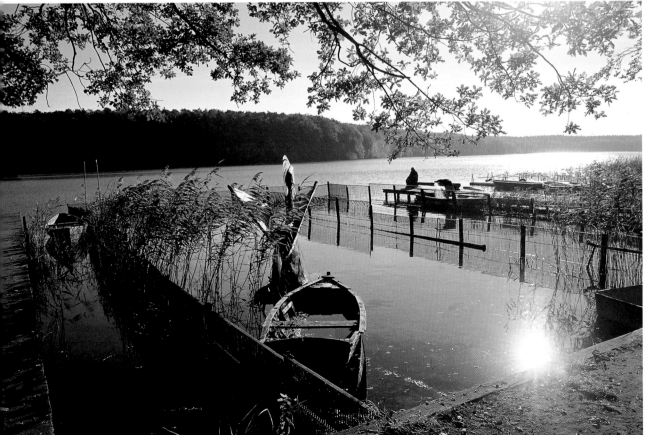

Above:
The system of sluices in Himmelpfort between the lakes Haus and Stolp was built in 1752, after which it was expanded and rebuilt a number of times. Inland shipping brought the region an economic upswing.

Left:
The Stechlin is the name of the late work of Theodor Fontane, an autobiographical novel full of humour and wisdom. Nevertheless, "the Stechlin" is mainly one of the most beautiful lakes in the state of Brandenburg.

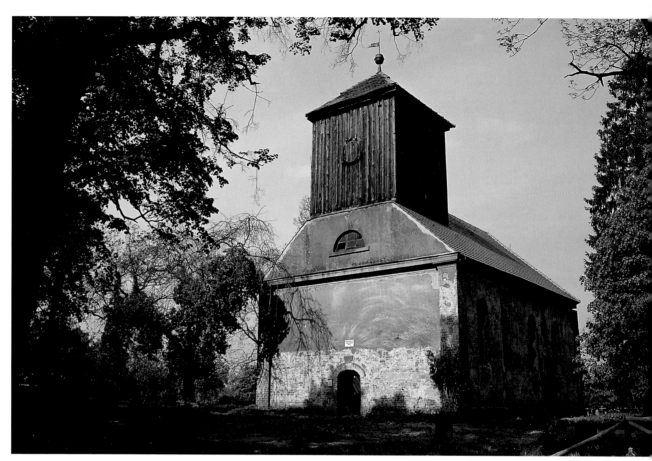

Right:
Küstrinchen – the name suits such a tiny town. Yet even villages have imposing churches. The Protestant house of worship dating from the mid-18th century stood empty for many years and is now partly restored.

Below:
A typical Brandenburg shot: a dock in Feldberg. The holiday resort is located in the charming Uckermark landscape with its over 400 lakes, its fields and broad beech forests, that practically beg you to come and hike, cycle and ride through them.

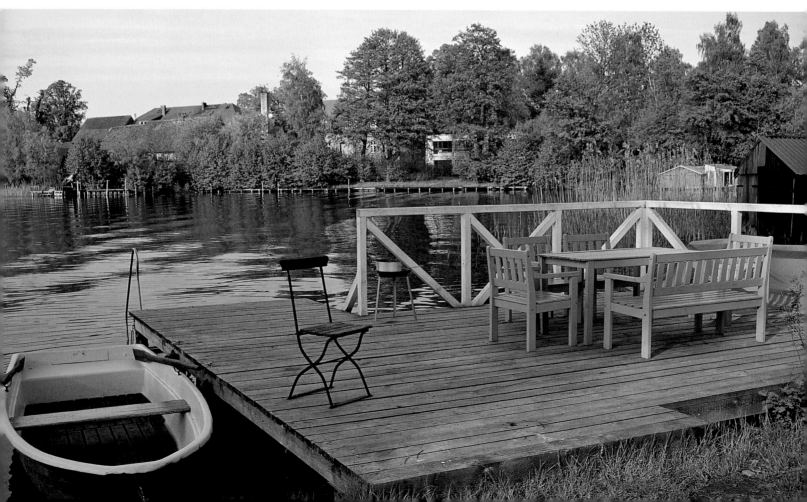

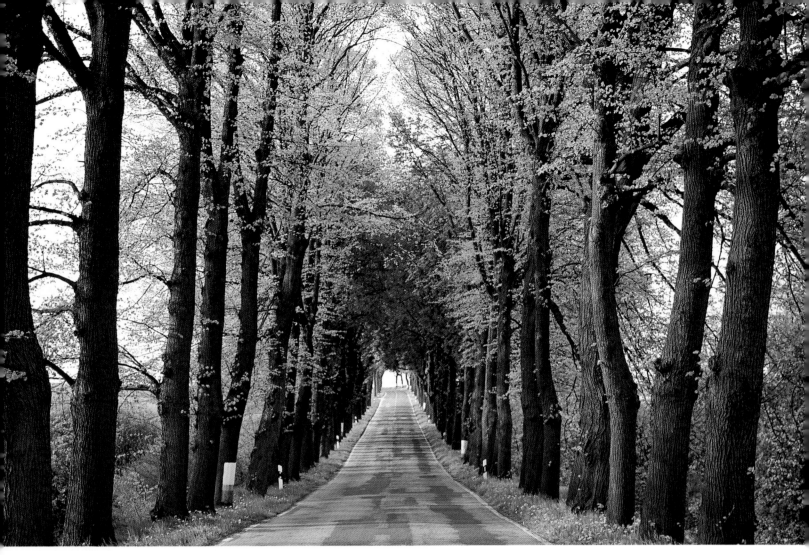

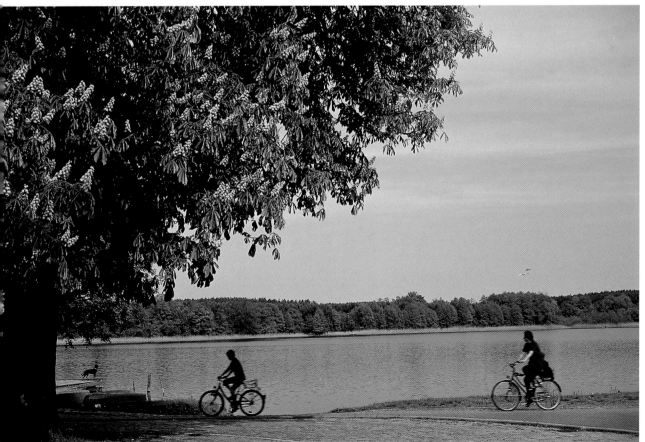

Above:
"Trees are poems that the earth writes upon the sky," said the poet Khalil Gibran. Brandenburg's famed tree-lined roads then are something like ballads with many verses. – This is one near Greifenberg.

Left:
Lychen calls itself "the town between the seven lakes." The state-accredited resort was the home of Johann Kirsten, a man to whom we owe a small, yet useful invention – the thumbtack!

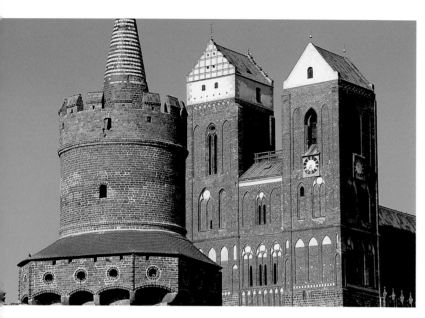

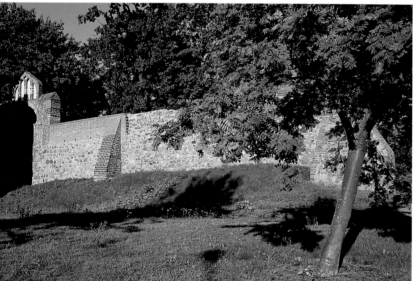

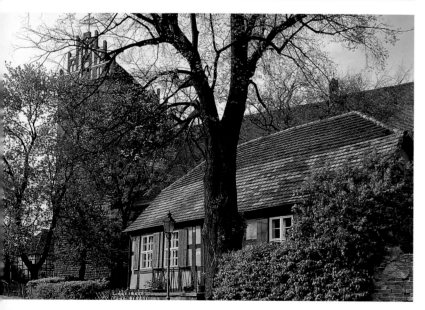

The Middle Gate Tower
and the Church of Mary
stand in Prenzlau. The
capital of the Uckermark
region has a plentiful
store of handsome brick
Gothic buildings.

Centre left:
On a city tour of Prenzlau,
we can discover gems of
the late middle ages. In
1287, the margrave him-
self granted permission

for the construction of
the nine meter (30 foot
high and two meter
(six foot)-thick city wa
with moats and emban
ments.

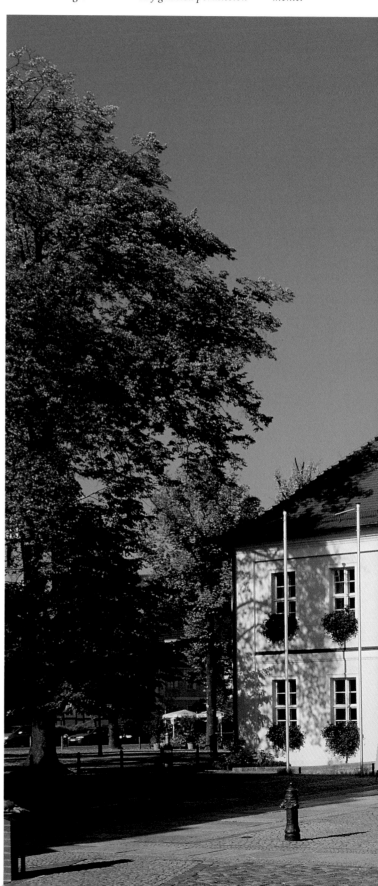

elow left:
he Romanesque-Gothic
urch of Mary in
ngermünde dates from
e 13th century. The
ree-aisled hall with its
llar vault shelters a
edieval treasure chest

and the remains of a
Renaissance altarpiece.
The Baroque organ was
built by the famous Berlin
organ builder Joachim
Wagner (1690–1749). It
has over 2,000 pipes and
is considered one of the

most beautifully sounding
instruments of Germany.
Organists from around
the world hold concerts
here. The organ's unique
features include two kettle-
drums played by angels.

Below:
In the historic city
centre of Angermünde is
the market square, sur-
rounded by the Baroque
town hall with Neo-

Classical facade and
enticing restaurants and
cafés in half-timbered
houses. The fountain on
the square was designed
by local artists.

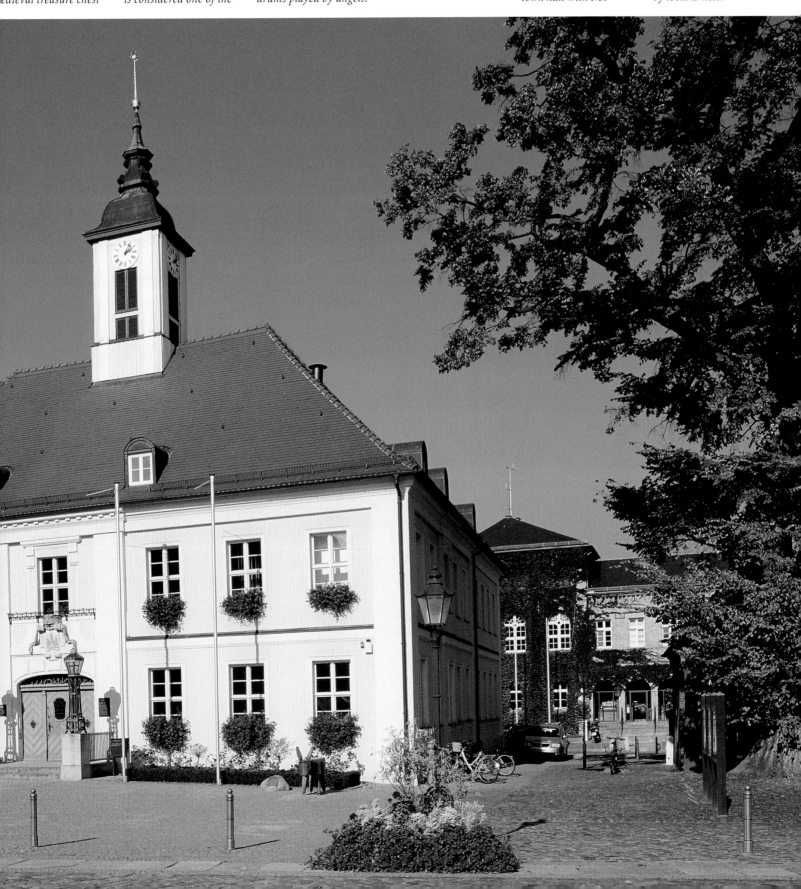

For eleven years, from 1933 to 1945, writer Rudolf Ditzen alias Hans Fallada, author of the worldwide success Little Man, What Now? lived in Carwitz – out in the country as he had always wished. Here, he hoped to find refuge from National Socialism and the chance for inner emigration. Here, he sought to offset his writing with work in the cow barn, threshing floor, apiary and potato fields. Yet, since he chose not to leave Nazi Germany, Fallada also experienced discrimination in Carwitz as a humanist writer.

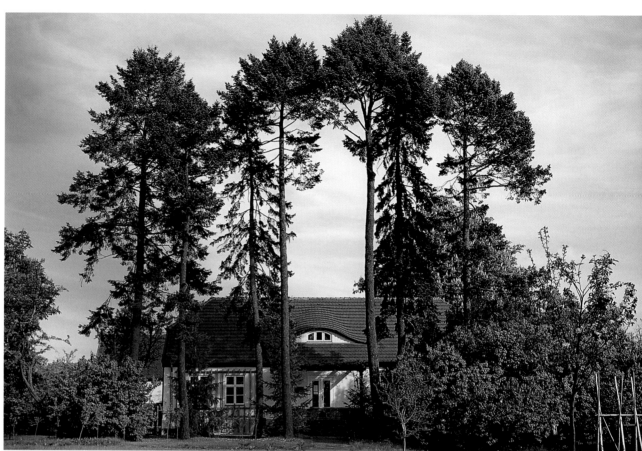

Castle ruin in Greifenberg. Not far from here is the village of Biesenbrow, where author Ehm Welk grew up. He writes of his home, the Uckermark: "Up there … is my country: a miles-wide, rectangular clod of earth whose deep green is hemmed on the eastern longitudinal side by the black of a range of hills and whose narrow sides to the south and north let the distance surge up as a velvety blue."

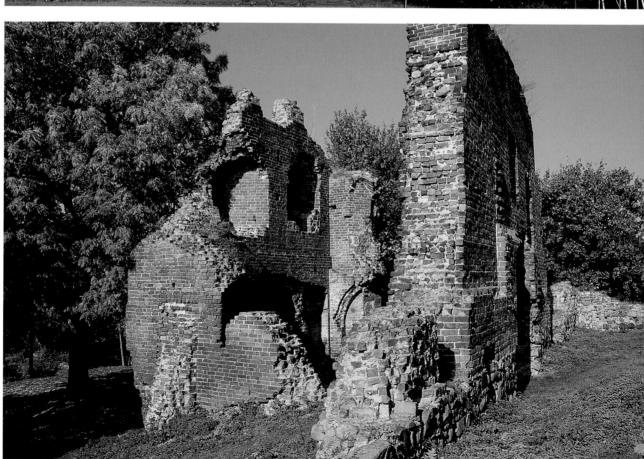

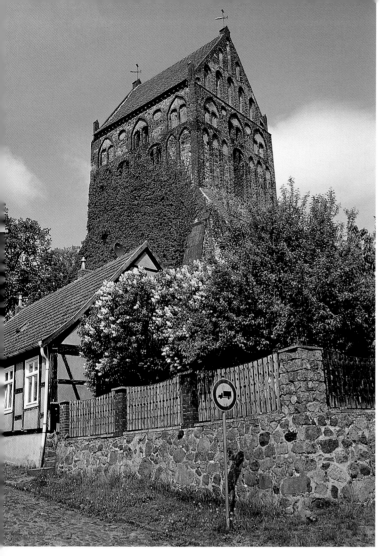

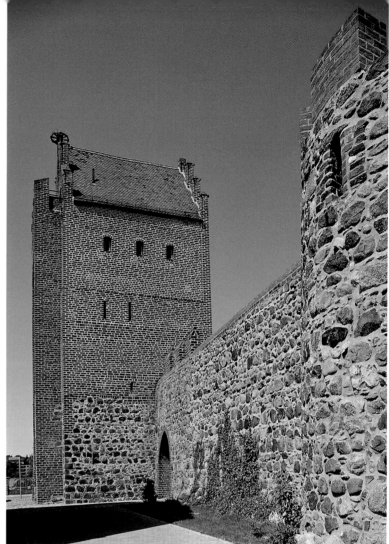

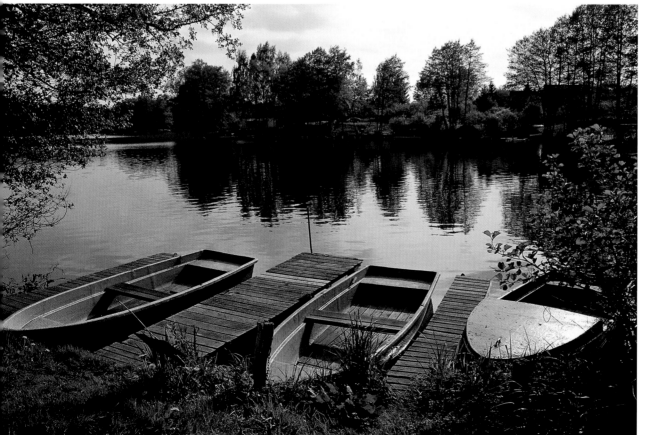

Above left:
Among the sights of Lychen are St. John's Church from the 13th century, the Baroque town hall and the rafting museum.

Above right:
The Berlin Gate of the Templin city wall today houses a permanent exhibition on the nature, landscape and biotopes of the Uckermark. Templin's medieval setting is better preserved than any other in the north.

Left:
Surrounded by dark green forests, on a narrow ridge between four lakes lies the village Carwitz, which was a fishing village as early as 1216. Today it is an idyllic place for people seeking peace and quiet.

113

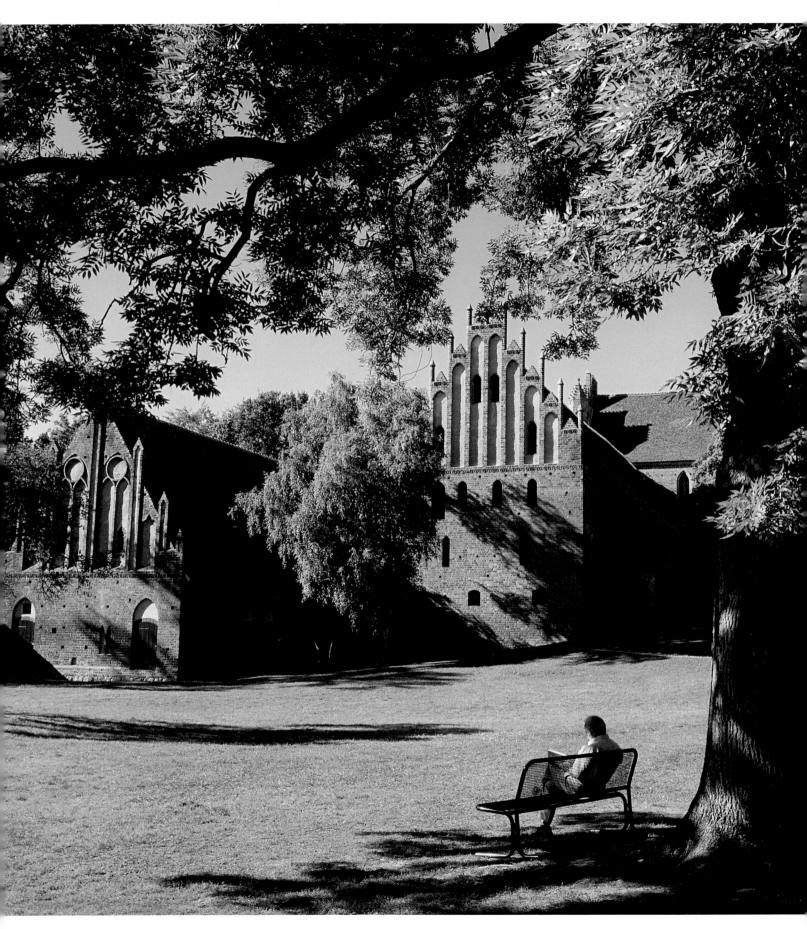

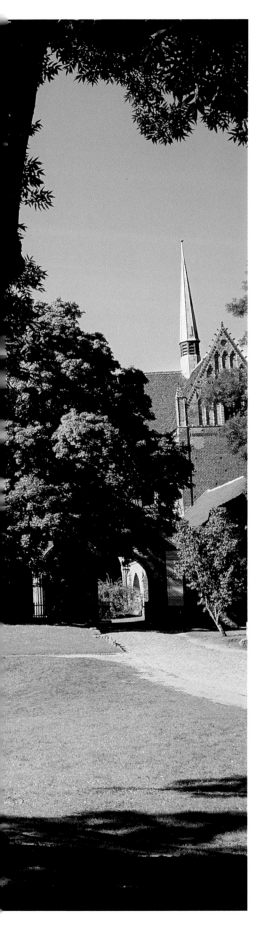

The unsettled history of Chorin monastery began in the 13th century. In its prime, the large complex was home to about seventy ordained monks and two hundred lay brothers of the Cistercian order. In 1542, the monastery had to be secularized. Over the following centuries the church and outbuildings were left to ruin, their stones were even quarried, until Karl Friedrich Schinkel initiated and asserted reconstruction in 1817. – A highlight for any journey in Brandenburg!

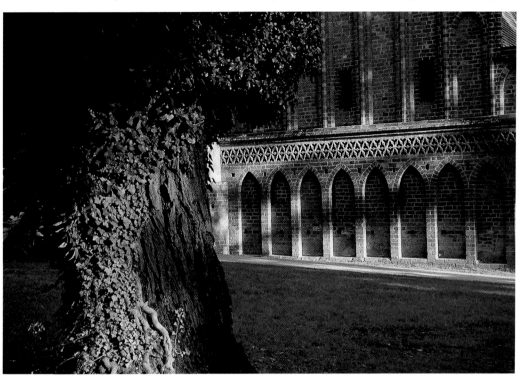

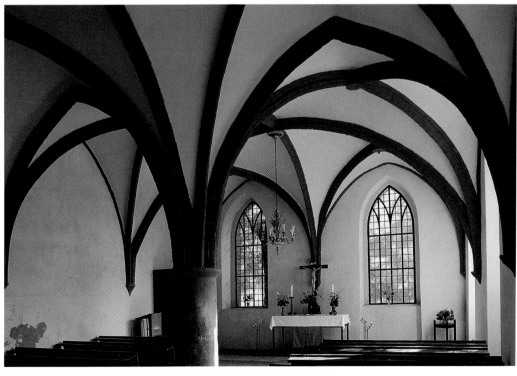

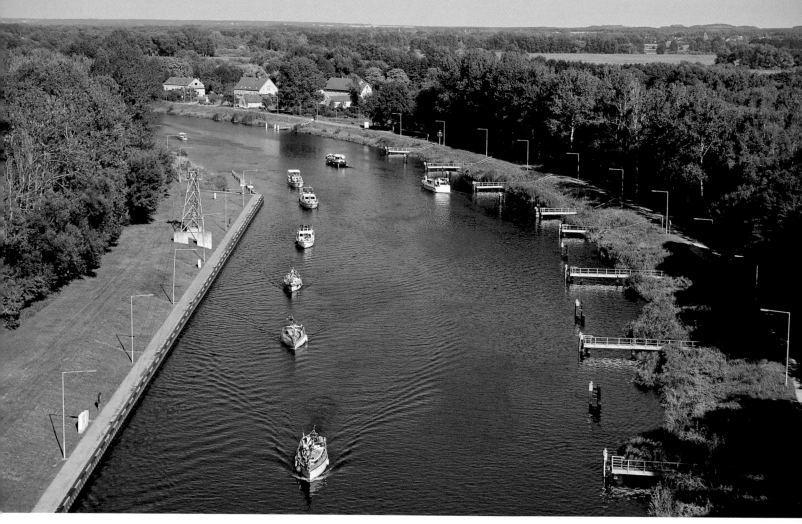

Above and right:
Canals were built as early as the 17th century to link the rivers Oder and Havel and make them navigable. To overcome differences in elevation, numerous sluices had to be passed through until 1934, when the ship lift was built in Niederfinow. In only five minutes, the ships are lifted 36 meters (118 feet); the entire procedure with ships entering and leaving the caisson takes about twenty minutes. Up to forty ships are lifted up or down here per day, transporting three million tonnes of goods every year. However, the Finow Canal is now so highly travelled that ships wait hours or even days for their turn in the lift.

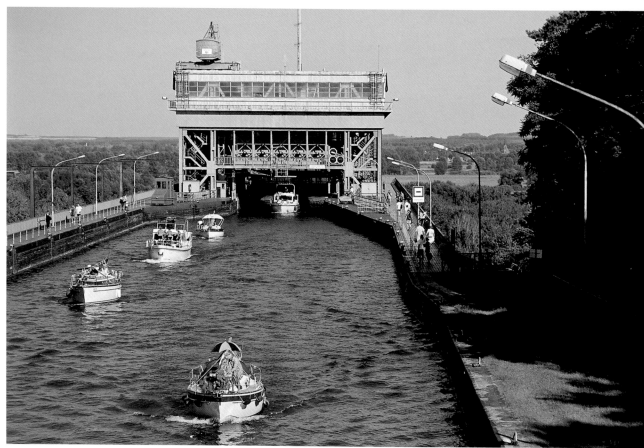

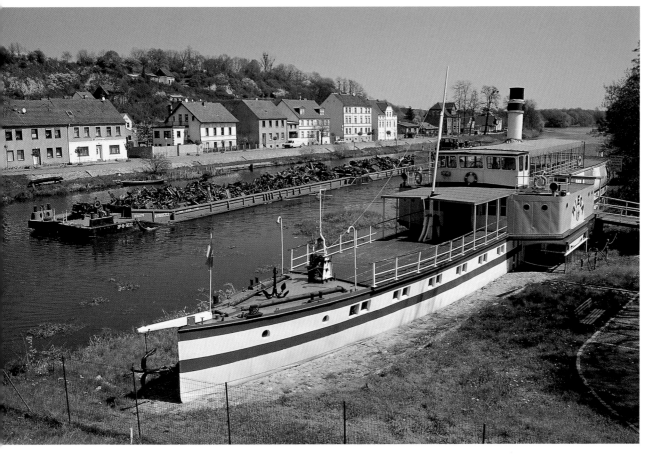

The largest and probably most famous exhibit piece of the Inland Shipping Museum in Oderberg is the paddle steamer "Riesa," built in 1897. On board the Riesa, visitors learn many interesting facts about steam shipping on the Oder.

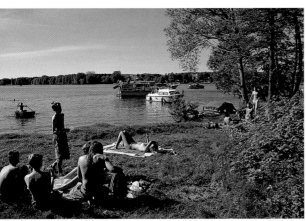

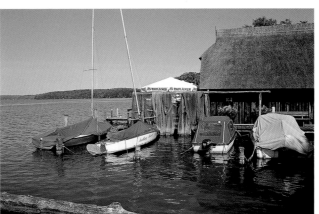

"The meadows take pleasure in the water," said the Chinese philosopher Confucius. Brandenburg has plenty of opportunities for taking such pleasure. The lakes Üder, Werbellin and Wandlitz invite us for a swim or a boat ride or just to take a rest on their shores.

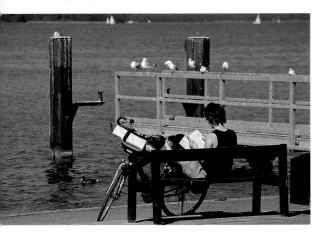

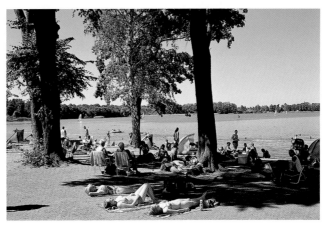

Right:

Wandlitz is known as the "forbidden city" of former East Germany's political elite: Walter Ulbricht and later Erich Honecker lived here amidst high government and party officials, yet shielded from common folk in what were actually modest, dreary postwar houses. Wandlitz still has its old village centre, however; before the war, the town was a popular day trip destination among Berliners.

Far right:

In the Schorfheide: the landmark of Glambeck, the Taubenturm (pigeon tower), houses an art gallery. The villagers began celebrating the Taubenturm festival every June in 1998.

Right:

To ensure that Kaiser Wilhelm II could reach his hunting grounds and his hunting lodge "Hubertusstock" ten kilometres (six miles) away undisturbed, in 1896 on the new Eberswalde-Templin railway line a stop was built just for him: the "Kaiserbahnhof" in Joachimsthal.

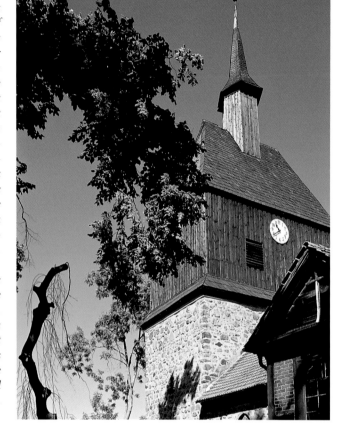

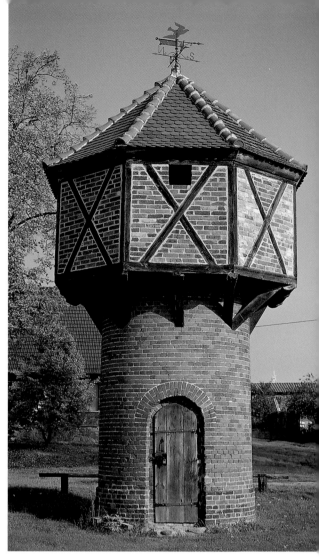

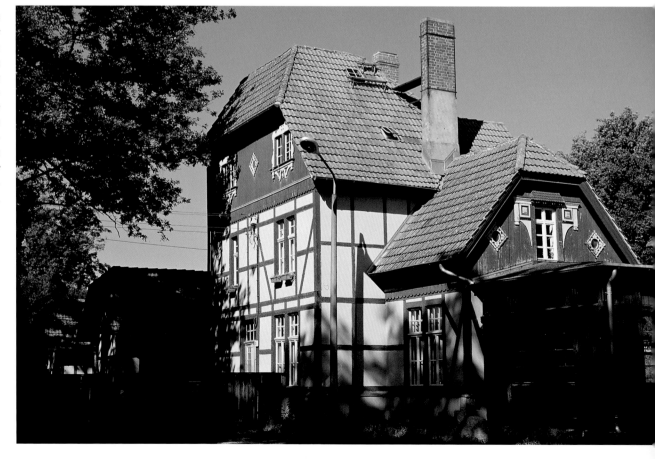

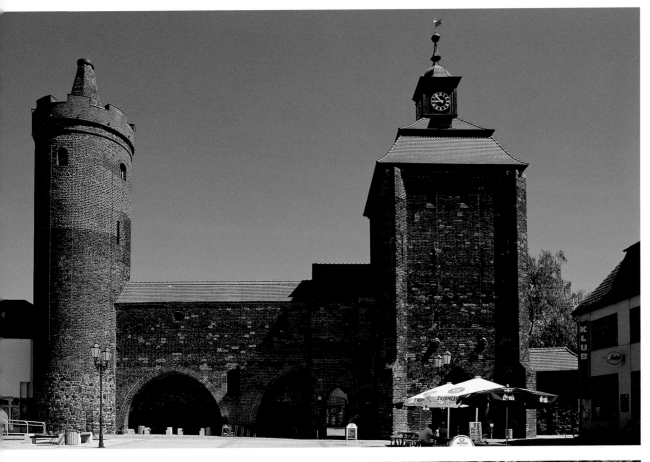

Bernau has a town wall dating from the 13th to 14th centuries, of which considerable parts are still extant, such as the Steintor gate, the Pulverturm and large parts of the embankments and moats.

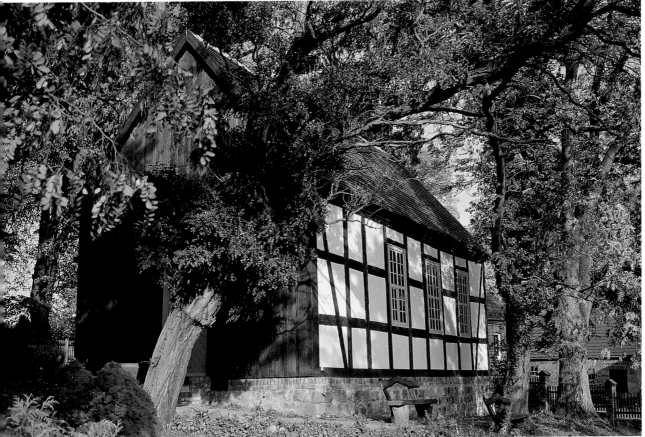

The little village of Glambeck is situated in the middle of the Schorfheide. The little half-timbered church was dedicated in 1708. After 1990, this rare "poor folks' church" was on the brink of complete ruin. Thanks to a number of initiatives, the structure could be saved. It was rededicated after two years of construction on 2 January 2000. Since then, the church has been used for sacred, cultural and tourism purposes, for concerts and exhibitions.

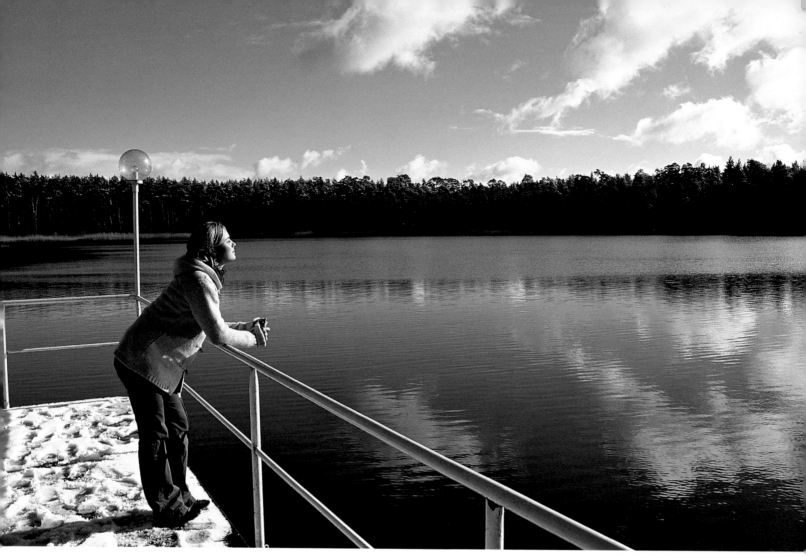

Above:
*Surrounded by the
enchanting landscape of
the Schorfheide-Chorin
biosphere reserve, the
town of Gross Dölln has
many opportunities for
relaxing, daydreaming
and enjoying life.*

Right:
*Winter on Lake Werbellin,
about sixty kilometres
(37 miles) from Berlin.
In 1981, the heads of
government of East and
West Germany, Erich
Honecker and Helmut
Schmidt, met in the hunt-
ing lodge on its shore. In
those days, the climate
between the systems
was icy. But, the political
thaw could not be
stopped …*

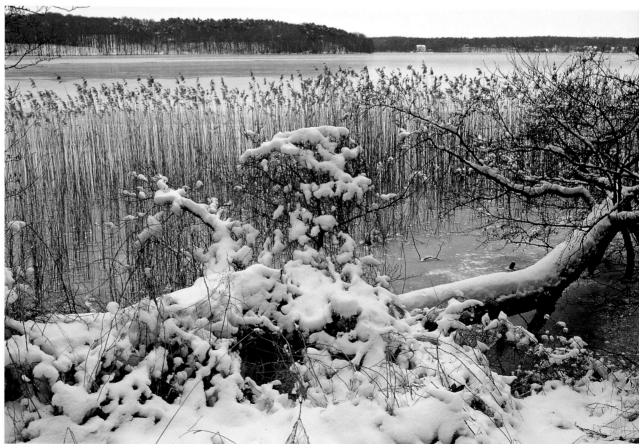

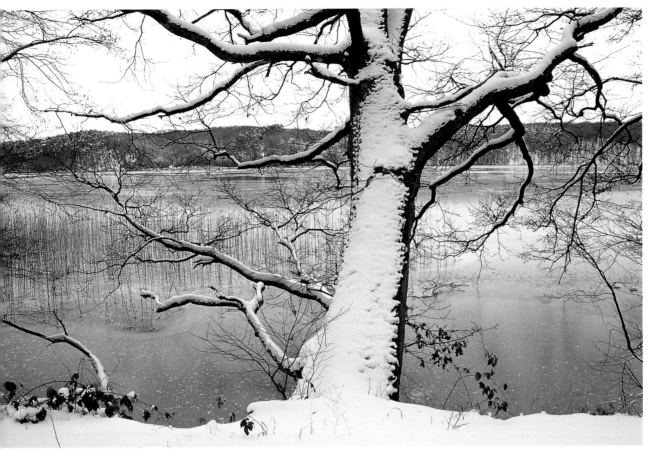

Left:
In the summer, Lake Werbellin is hardly isolated; it's the realm of hikers and water sports enthusiasts. In the winter, the lake has a special charm described and celebrated in song by many poets over the ages.

Below:
"In harsh winters the partridges sat close by the barns," wrote Peter Huchel, called the lyrical voice of Brandenburg. His poem "My Grandfather" ends: "He turned the brass ring of the lamp. / The sun began to glimmer, / the jay screamed / and flew into the cold march morning." – Impression of Lake Dölln.

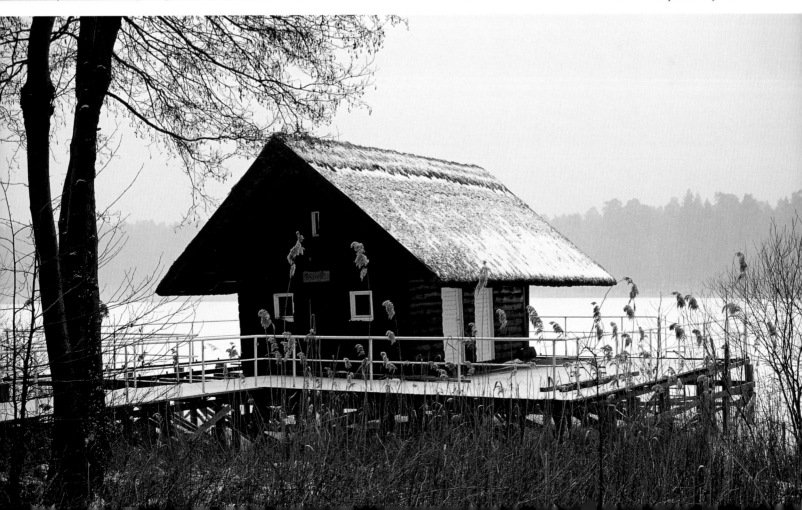

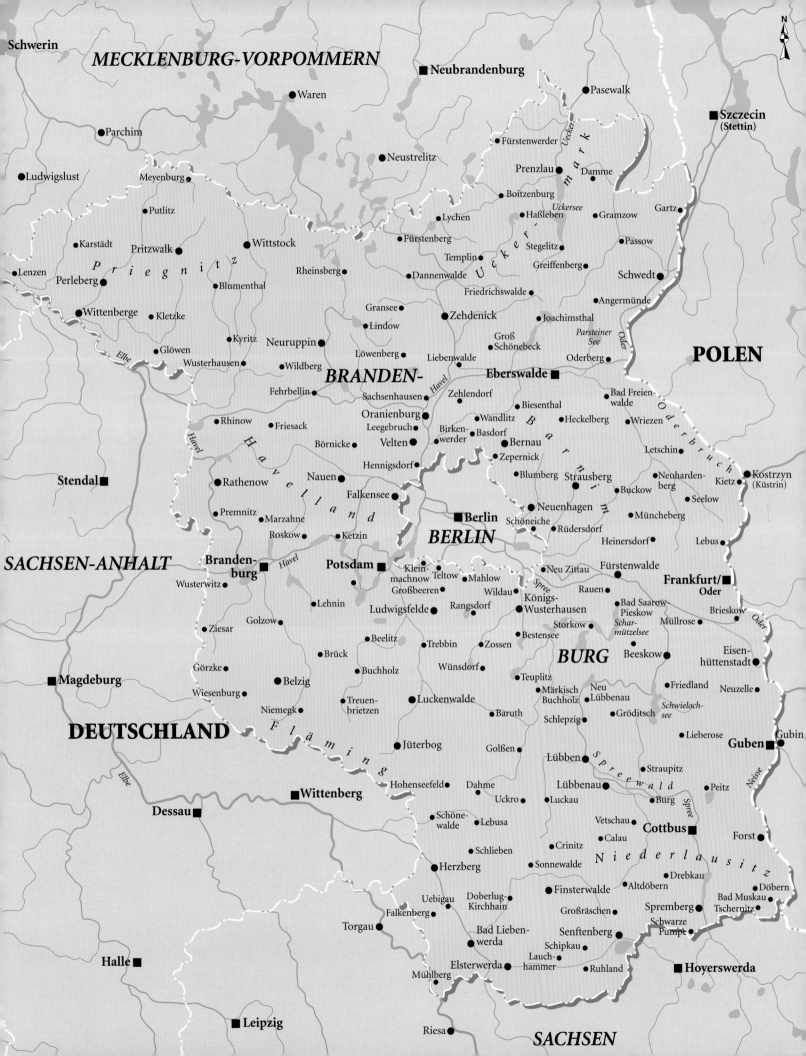

Theodor Fontane answers the question whether one should take a journey through the Mark Brandenburg: "Go ahead, you will not regret it. Inimitable joys and pleasures shall accompany you." – An outing on one of the many lakes is one such pleasure: the boat rocks gently as you survey the smooth surface of the water while time seems to stand still. So simple, so good...

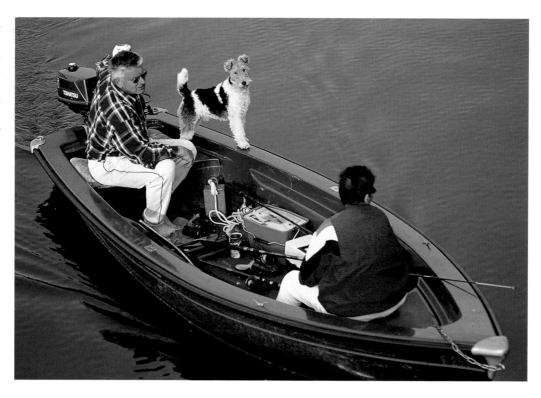

Credits

Book design
hoyerdesign grafik gmbh, Freiburg

Map
Fischer Kartografie, Fürstenfeldbruck

Translation
Faith Gibson Tegethoff, Swisttal

Printed in Germany
Repro: Artilitho, Trento, Italy
Printed/Bound by: Offizin Andersen Nexö, Leipzig
© 2006 Verlagshaus Würzburg GmbH & Co. KG
© Photos: Wolfgang Korall

ISBN-13: 978-3-8003-1707-3
ISBN-10:   3-8003-1707-9

Look for our complete programme at:
www.verlagshaus.com

The photographer
Wolfgang Korall, *born 1949 in Thuringia, lives and works as a photographer in Berlin. As a specialist for Germany and Eastern Europe, he has published many travel books, picture books and calendars. He has contributed to books about East Prussia, the Mazurskie Lakeland and Silesia for Verlagshaus Würzburg.*

The author
Georg Schwikart, *born in 1964, lives in Sankt Augustin near Bonn where he works as a freelance author and publicist. In addition to his many books and articles for anthologies, newspapers and magazines, he also writes for radio and television. He has contributed to books about Egypt, Brittany, Rome and Turkey for Verlagshaus Würzburg.*

Stürtz

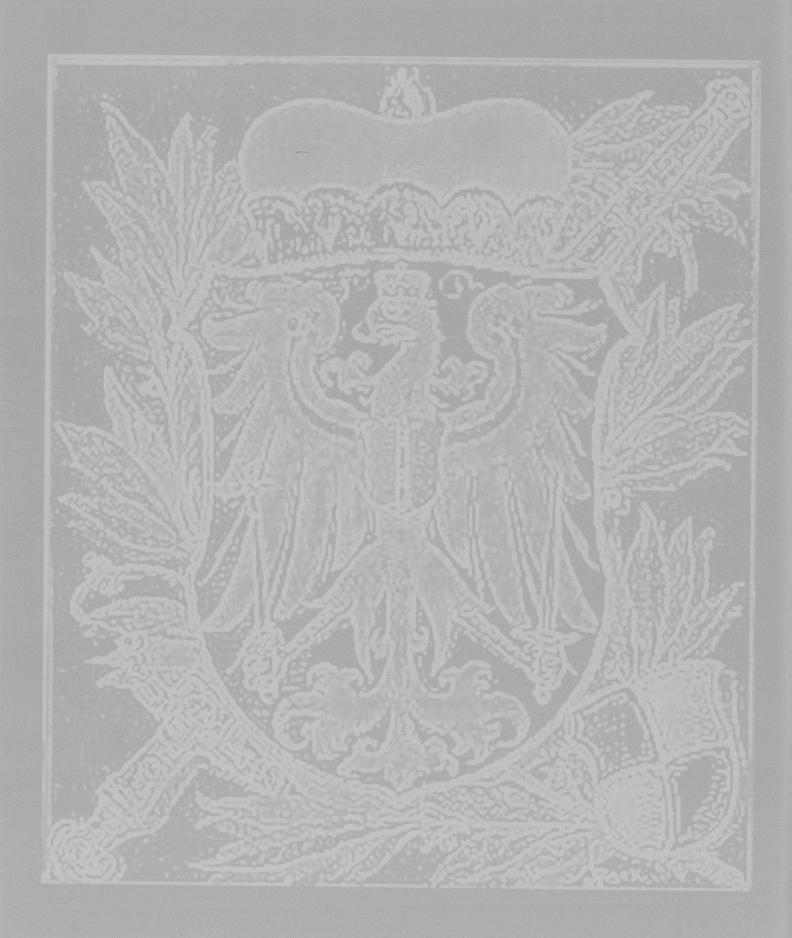